# A City Full of Hawks

## *On the Waterfront* Seventy Years Later— Still the Great American Contender

Stephen Rebello

**APPLAUSE**
THEATRE & CINEMA BOOKS

**APPLAUSE**
**THEATRE & CINEMA BOOKS**

Bloomsbury Publishing Group, Inc.
4501 Forbes Blvd., Ste. 200
Lanham, MD 20706
ApplauseBooks.com

Distributed by NATIONAL BOOK NETWORK

**Library of Congress Cataloging-in-Publication Data**

Names: Rebello, Stephen, author.
Title: A city full of hawks : On the waterfront seventy years later-still
    the great American contender / Stephen Rebello.
Description: Essex, Connecticut : Applause, [2024] | Includes
    bibliographical references and index. | Summary: "Perhaps no movie has
    better captured the interplay of ambition, corruption, and
    disappointment in America than On the Waterfront, best captured in the
    closing "I could've been a contender" speech given by Marlon Brando's
    character Terry Malloy. A gripping tale about organized crime and
    dockworkers in New Jersey, it ist justifiably remembered today as one of
    the greatest movies of the twentieth century. This film about
    internecine power struggles and thwarted ambition had its share of big
    personalities involved in its making, among them Brando, Elia Kazan,
    playwright Arthur Miller, screenwriter Schulberg, producer Sam Spiegel,
    composer Leonard Bernstein, Marilyn Monroe, Rod Steiger, Eva Marie
    Saint, Paul Newman, Joanne Woodward, Frank Sinatra, Elizabeth
    Montgomery, Grace Kelly, Aaron Copland, Martin Scorsese, and more. What
    happened among them, let alone the dramas that were unfolding in their
    personal lives when they were off set, ironically recalls Michael
    Corleone says in one of On the Waterfront's most celebrated descendents,
    The Godfather: "It's not personal. It's strictly business." But, of
    course, it's always intensely personal-as Stephen Rebello's fascinating
    narrative of the film's making shows"— Provided by publisher.
Identifiers: LCCN 2024011834 (print) | LCCN 2024011835 (ebook) | ISBN
    9781493077809 (cloth) | ISBN 9781493077816 (epub)
Subjects: LCSH: On the waterfront (Motion picture) | Kazan, Elia—Criticism
    and interpretation. | Crime films—United States—History and criticism.
    | Motion pictures—Production and direction—United
    States—History—20th century.
Classification: LCC PN1997.O43 R43 2024  (print) | LCC PN1997.O43 (ebook)
    | DDC 791.43/42—dc23/eng/20240708
LC record available at https://lccn.loc.gov/2024011834
LC ebook record available at https://lccn.loc.gov/2024011835

♾™ The paper used in this publication meets the minimum requirements of
American National Standard for Information Sciences—Permanence of Paper for
Printed Library Materials, ANSI/NISO Z39.48-1992

*For my father, Arthur, who walked the walk.*

Terry Malloy: "You know this city's full of hawks? That's a fact. They hang around on the top of the big hotels. And they spot a pigeon in the park. Right down on them."

—Budd Schulberg, On the Waterfront

# Contents

# Acknowledgments

There are so many people to thank for the existence of this labor of love. To my agent, Lee Sobel, I owe so much for fanning the long-smoldering spark that led to my finally writing it. Deep appreciation goes to John Cerullo, an erudite prince among editors at Applause Books, for his intelligence, good taste, and enthusiasm.

For the time and insights they graciously shared, the kindnesses small and mighty alike, my gratitude goes out to Alec Baldwin, Arthur Miller, Eva Marie Saint, Budd Schulberg, Martin Scorsese, Steven C. Smith, Marc von Arx, Bob Crewe, Betty Spiegel, Pen Densham, and John Watson.

A million thanks to Joseph Veltre of The Gersh Agency for his gracious and expert stewardship of the Budd Schulberg estate.

The world is a better place because of people who refuse to stand down in the face of injustice. Here's to the people in my life who contributed so much to the person I am today, beginning with my parents, who stood on the right side of history, even if it was unpopular.

Nothing but gratitude to those in my life who beamed with enthusiasm any time I told them about my progress on this book, including Gary Rubenstein, Howard and Steinunn Green, Deborah Corday, Dr. Tod Tams, Kathy Silva, and Eileen Young. You mean more to me than you may ever know.

To those who still aspire to make art that matters, that touches the heart and soul, that helps lift and change the world, you inspire me every day.

And, finally, my endless love and appreciation to Buster, for demonstrating why people willingly go to the ends of the earth for those they love.

# Preface

*"A son has to finally kill his father, doesn't he?"*

—Elia Kazan

**A** confession. I came to *On the Waterfront* the long, long way around. And not especially willingly.

I was too young to see the film when it first stormed theaters in 1954, garnering reverential reviews and planting the flag for a new wave of naturalistic acting and stripped-down moviemaking. As a moviegoer coming of age in the 1960s and 1970s, I had plenty of opportunities to catch up with *On the Waterfront* when it resurfaced on television or in revival theaters. But I let them pass me by. In the popular culture back then, it seemed as though almost everybody knew the movie's signature line "I coulda been a contender" whether they'd heard it spoken by Marlon Brando in the film itself or by one of the dozens of celebrity impressionists popular at the time. Still, once I finally saw the movie, it dawned on me that I had been avoiding it. It took time for me to grapple with the complicated reasons why. But more about that later.

By the late 1970s, I had read and heard so much about *On the Waterfront* that I felt like I'd already been there and done that. I knew that the movie had caught 1950s audiences up short with its gritty, documentary-style New Jersey locations and European neo-realist movie influences. How could it not strike like lightning when it opened against such other late-summer fare as the biblical costume spectacle *Demetrius and the Gladiators*; the gloriously subversive suburban romance of young playboy Rock Hudson and lovestruck middle-aged widow Jane Wyman in *Magnificent Obsession*; the mass attacks by gigantic, irradiated ants in *Them!*; or the hammy histrionics of the bloated airborne disaster epic *The High and the Mighty*?

I knew that *On the Waterfront* had swept its Oscar season and that, after America had been rocked by years of the House Un-American Activities Committee's (HUAC) hunting for alleged communists and infiltrators in Hollywood, it defied logic by becoming a box-office success—even though its esteemed director, Elia Kazan, and screenwriter, Budd Schulberg, were among those who named names of friends who'd joined the Communist Party decades before, getting them blacklisted or preventing them from working. Because the movie challenged audiences with thorny questions of loyalty, guilt, conscience, betrayal, and speaking truth to power, it was an anomaly in the Eisenhower 1950s. For decades, critics had been praising the raw immediacy of the performances delivered by the Actors Studio ensemble cast of Eva Marie Saint, Karl Malden, and Lee J. Cobb—with Marlon Brando contributing a titanic Stanislavskian turn as an isolated, undereducated, failed prizefighter turned longshoreman struggling to reclaim some measure of honor and dignity by blowing the whistle on a venal and corrupt waterfront boss. With all this going for it, why did I wait roughly a quarter century after the film's release to finally catch up with it?

At first, I chalked up my dodging *On the Waterfront* to timing. For my teenage self, art was what spoke to me and my generation— *A Hard Day's Night*, Thomas McGuane, The Velvet Underground, *Bonnie and Clyde*, Dylan, The Byrds and *The Birds*, Herman Hesse, James Baldwin, Joan Didion, *Blow-Up*, Leonard Cohen, James Brown, *Rosemary's Baby*, *McCabe & Mrs. Miller*, Phil Ochs, *Belle de*

*Jour, If. . . .*, and *That Was the Week That Was*. But along with them was my big yes to Natalie Wood's, Warren Beatty's, and Barbara Loden's full-throttle emotionality in *Splendor in the Grass*. You see, I wasn't oblivious to Kazan, having also read Arthur Miller's *Death of a Salesman* and Tennessee Williams's *A Streetcar Named Desire* as a high schooler, knowing of Kazan's legendary Broadway stage productions, plus loving his, Brando's, and Vivien Leigh's electrifying movie version of the latter. I even recall my know-it-all preteen 1960s self, sitting at the far end of my parents' taupe-colored sectional sofa in our suburban southeastern New England home watching Kazan-directed movies on TV, like *Pinky*, *A Tree Grows in Brooklyn*, *Gentlemen's Agreement*, and even *Man on a Tightrope* and *Viva Zapata!* But still no *On the Waterfront*.

Two things helped move the needle.

Sometime in 1968, I came across a newspaper story announcing how Kazan would soon be directing Marlon Brando, Faye Dunaway, and Deborah Kerr in the film version of his bestselling novel *The Arrangement*, which he said had something to do with "a man who has to kill himself to be born again" and "the shivery, trembling affluence of America along with the self-disgust and bewilderment that are so common here." All this lofty talk and Kazan's promise of nudity and salty language, never mind a theme song especially written for the movie by Joni Mitchell? As both a Mitchell acolyte and a devotee of overheated melodrama the likes of *Written on the Wind* and *Strangers When We Meet*, much less the earlier-mentioned *Splendor in the Grass*, *The Arrangement* sounded, especially after I had read Kazan's novel, like a big, gooey ice cream sundae of angst and sex. Something *On the Waterfront*, for all its apparent brilliance, had never sounded like to me. Sadly, whatever over-the-top fun *The Arrangement* might have had vanished, along with Marlon Brando and Joni Mitchell's rejected theme song, from Kazan's vilified 1969 movie version. But Kazan suddenly did become contemporary enough for me to think seriously about finally getting *On the Water-front* off the "should see" category. Still, I slept on it.

Early fall, 1973. An old high school buddy, studying at Emerson College in Boston, Massachusetts, invites me to a top-secret private screening of a new crime movie winning pre-release raves. Do I want to join him? I do. The film turns out to be *Mean Streets*, an edgy, violent, wild ride directed by an up-and-comer named Martin Scorsese and starring two new (to me) fireballs, Robert De Niro and Harvey Keitel. Almost from the first frame, my enthusiasm for the movie—and that of the others lucky to be there—could have scorched the theater. Afterward, the savvy young movie guru who set up the screening chatted about how much he loved the movie and noted that although Scorsese's work felt entirely new, it was also reminiscent of the Italian neorealism movement of the 1940s and 1950s and *On the Waterfront*. That did it.

A few months later, I went alone to a revival theater of a Brando double bill of *On the Waterfront* and *The Wild One*. By the fadeout of *Waterfront*, I could barely move from my seat. The gale force of Brando's brutish, poetic, moving performance? Definitive. I finally got it together enough to leave the theater, went out for a quick bite, then doubled backed to the theater to experience *Waterfront* all over again.

Only then did it dawn on me why I had kept away from the film for so long. The urban setting, the compelling authenticity of the exploited real-life longshoremen Kazan used in the movie, Brando's character's moral quandary and decision to call out injustice despite the personal cost, they all cut close to home. My father, a sometimes inarticulate, moody man with a gentle soul and a huge heart, spent over 25 years of his life working a waterfront mill job at a tire and rubber plant that had opened in the 1920s. The city was virtually built around it, and with several thousand employees working around the clock, it became the nation's biggest supplier of rubber goods. Although a loyal union member and anything but a rabble-rouser, my dad grew angry and frustrated at seeing himself and his coworkers overworked, underpaid, unprotected from serious injuries on the job, and underserved by their union. He became a vocal and influential member of a group of workers advocating for a major walkout that brought production to a standstill. As the strike wore on and the management hired "scabs" to replace the strikers, tempers flared, and workers feared they would lose their jobs, homes, and livelihoods as the strike wore on and "scabs" replaced the strikers. My dad lost friends and received threatening phone calls. My parents suffered sleepless nights and took second jobs, and we ate lots of leftovers. On the picket line, my dad and his fellow strikers were heckled and mocked. In the supermarket, a neighbor asked if we'd turn "communist." We'd wake up to find our trash cans overturned, and our driveway was littered with rusty nails. I never saw my father more vulnerable or more resolute. I was never prouder of him.

The strike ended with the management offering little in the way of reforms. My dad went back to work, but his loyalty to the company and the labor union was crushed. A very few years later, the factory shut down practically overnight and decamped to a more amenable locale. The local economy was decimated, with over 1,300 workers jobless and without pensions. In subsequent years, my father refused to talk much about his brush with activism. He told me once that he didn't regret the stand he had taken because he had searched his conscience and acted on what he believed was fair and just. We once watched *On the Waterfront* together on television. At the end of the ardently anti-union movie, I saw him brush away tears. Later, he toughened up and said, "Here's how you know it's just a fairy tale: it expects you to believe that Brando's actions will change things for the better and that the mob won't punish him. What a crock. What he did won't mean a damn thing, and they'll get him in the end."

*On the Waterfront* became all that much more personal to me. In 1991, it became even more so when I was busy writing magazine features between books and film scripts. The editors of *Movieline* magazine asked if I was interested in interviewing gifted playwright and screenwriter Nicholas Kazan, known for his work on such movies as *Frances*, let alone his Oscar-nominated *Reversal of Fortune* screenplay. I said yes in a heartbeat because I'd already included two of his scripts in the "Ten Best Unproduced Screenplays" *American Film* and *Movieline* feature stories for which I canvassed fellow writers as well as trusted development executives, producers, directors, actors, and agents, many of whom had commended Kazan's work. One studio executive said, "I'm sure you know that Nick's not only a major talent, but he's also the son of Elia Kazan, so when you talk with him, expect some sensitivity about talking about his father." In Elia Kazan's 1988 autobiography *Elia Kazan: A Life*, the younger Kazan barely gets much mention aside from being called "new one" when he came into the world. And indeed, in Nicholas Kazan's unproduced screenplay *Punk Daddy*, a guy snuffs his despised father and stuffs the corpse in a sofa. In *At Close Range* (filmed in 1986 and starring Sean Penn and Christopher Walken; for my money, Kazan's script remains unproduced), a charming sociopathic dad tries to slaughter his kids after luring them into a crime spree. Nick told me, "I used to believe that my father was jealous or wary of my success because he felt in some sense that he was being replaced. After every film of mine, he'd say, 'Better luck next time.' When he read *At Close Range*, he said, 'Boy, this is good. I hope they do it.' When he went to see the movie, he wrote me a letter blaming me for all its faults. I said, 'If that's what you thought, why didn't you tell me when you read the script?'"

It was with Nick (not only a neighbor of mine at the time but who also turned out to be a brilliant, funny guy) whom Elia Kazan stayed during his time in Los Angeles to receive his hugely controversial honorary Oscar in 1999. Knowing that the elderly Kazan was still raging over how he believed Hollywood had misunderstood and mistreated him since *On the Waterfront*—made as an allegory but not an apologia—made me wonder if I should immediately consider writing a book about the making of the film and its aftermath. I'm glad that I've waited. It would have been a much different book by a different person.

I hope to immerse you in every phase of the creation of one of the greatest, most important, and enduring movies ever made, featuring a towering central performance of such magnitude and genius that its impact and influence are still being felt today. It's a portrait of a group of talented, brave, flawed, all-too-human men and women coming together and—despite the odds—creating art that is very much of its time and yet timeless. What does *On the Waterfront*, a movie that deals so earnestly and messily with themes of conscience, guilt, personal redemption, honor, corruption, and self-deception, have to say to our post-truth era? Does *On the Waterfront*—not to mention its themes—matter any longer? I think so. Let's find out together.

# ONE

# They Cover the Waterfront

## *It Starts with Johnson and Siodmak*

In June 1949, Joseph Curtis, head of advertising and publicity for the independent movie company Monticello Film Corporation, surprised larger-than-life, swashbuckling investigative journalist Malcolm Johnson by expressing his interest in optioning the motion picture rights to Johnson's 24 "Crime on the Waterfront" articles published November and December 1948 in the *New York Sun*. Johnson's reportage exposed how, under the aegis of the International Longshoremen's Association's (ILA's) president, Joseph Ryan, in league with such others as Meyer Lansky and Albert "Mad Hatter" Anastasia, the waterfront and its unions were firmly under the thumb of organized crime. After Johnson won the Pulitzer Prize, the *Sun* and other New York newspapers reported that Johnson had struck a deal with Curtis and Monticello, a company specifically focused on tracking and acquiring newspapers and magazine stories with film potential. The *Sun* article reported that the movie to be made from Johnson's articles would be a full-length dramatic feature done in documentary style. Curtis's intention to take a gritty, edgy, newsreel-influenced approach to dramatizing Johnson's material makes sense given the blunt force of Johnson's work.

Post–World War II audiences for international cinema were responding to the growing influence of the Italian neorealism movement, typified by the 1940s work of such filmmakers as Luchino Visconti, Vittorio De Sica, and Roberto Rossellini in their films *Ossessione*, *Bicycle Thieves*, and *Rome, Open City*, respectively. Those works had begun making their mark on American filmmakers, including Billy Wilder with *Lost Weekend* and *The House on 92nd Street*, directed by Henry Hathaway. Its impact was particularly apparent on the visual style, mood, and ambience of some of the melodramas made from the work of such maestros of hard-boiled fiction as Dashiell Hammett, Raymond Chandler, and James M. Cain.

None of this was lost on Joseph Curtis. Not only was he the son of Jack Cohn, cofounder and executive vice president of Columbia Pictures, who ran Columbia's New York office, but he was also the nephew of Harry Cohn, Columbia's notoriously crass, penny-pinching Hollywood-based production head, who in the 1930s and 1940s rescued the company from its Poverty Row past to become the home base of director Frank Capra's Oscar-sweeping 1934 comedy *It Happened One Night*. Cohn leveraged that success with such prestigious and audience-pleasing successors as *Mr. Smith Goes to Washington*, *Holiday*, *Gilda*, and more. In good times and bad, competition and enmity raged for decades between the brothers Cohn. Jack had more than once tried and failed to boot his older brother, known for such witticisms as "I don't get ulcers, I give them" and for judging a good movie as one that "doesn't make my ass squirm," from the company. Cohn's remark prompted *Citizen Kane* screenwriter Herman J. Mankiewicz to quip, "Imagine, the whole world wired to Harry Cohn's ass!" What's more, Curtis's brother, Robert, ran Columbia's offices in Paris and later became a film studio production executive. By 1949, Curtis's other brother, Ralph, was urging Columbia to muscle into television; successful in his mission to retool Screen Gems, the company's syndicated animation component, into a television production studio. By 1954, Screen Gems was turning out such gold-mine TV series as *Father Knows Best* and *The Adventures of Rin-Tin-Tin* as well as leasing to television Columbia's backlog of feature film releases and syndicating shorts starring the Three Stooges.

In late 1949, Curtis got bumped up from Monticello's head of advertising and publicity to company president. With that promotion, he began hiring and firing a succession of screenwriters who were in the process of attempting to create something filmic out of Malcolm Johnson's waterfront corruption exposés. Things clicked once Curtis joined forces with German émigré film director Robert Siodmak, who had been making swift, assured, tightly budgeted Hollywood movies since 1939, most often under a long-term contract with Universal. His Expressionist sensibilities were especially attuned to fatalistic thrillers and nasty crime melodramas, including *Phantom Lady*, *The Strange Affair of Uncle Harry*, *The Spiral Staircase*, *The File on Thelma Jordan*, and *The Killers*, the latter his sole Oscar-nominated directing gig and one that made stars out of Burt Lancaster and Ava Gardner. But many of Siodmak's best career opportunities were behind him. And having worked since the 1930s on screenplays for his films, though only occasionally receiving story credit for such work as the 1945 Humphrey Bogart psychological melodrama *Conflict*, he sparked to the dramatic and filmic possibilities in Johnson's raw material.

Casting about for the right screenwriter, Siodmak aggressively pursued Budd Schulberg. The 34-year-old Schulberg had become a household name with the 1941 publication of *What Makes Sammy Run*, his mordant yet humane dissection of the rise and fall of a relentlessly ambitious young Lower East Side–born hustler who lies, cheats, and steals his way to the top of the Hollywood mountain. Schulberg modeled his antihero after his father B. P. Schulberg, a giant and early Hollywood visionary, who from 1925 to 1932 was the

West Coast production head of the prestigious Paramount Pictures. Among Schulberg's canniest creative and commercial glories at Paramount, where he was paid $12,000 per week, was promoting major talent, including first-rate directors Ernst Lubitsch, Josef von Sternberg, Rouben Mamoulian, and William A. Wellman, much less such stars as Clara Bow, Cary Grant, Marlene Dietrich, Gilbert Roland, William Powell, and Maurice Chevalier. No wonder birthday parties for Budd, his shy, fiercely intelligent young son afflicted with a crippling stammer, were dutifully attended by heartthrob Rudolph Valentino as well as by the child stars Shirley Temple and Mitzi Green, who seemed about as happy to be there as the rented ponies and alligators. With a father that powerful, it isn't surprising that "It" Girl Clara Bow vamped little Budd or that his burst of laughter caused an expensive retake on a Marx Brothers movie set.

By the time of his 10th birthday, Schulberg had lots of boxer friends. He'd been going twice a week to the fights with his dad at the Hollywood Legion Stadium, down on El Centro Avenue in Los Angeles. Schulberg once referred to the place as "the social center of the town" in those days. Said Schulberg, "Since my father was a big shot and running a studio, the fighters would come out to visit. So very early on I got to know them, and I've always been attracted to them. There's something special about boxing to me."

Robert Siodmak and Joseph Curtis trekked out to Budd Schulberg's home, a sprawling working farm in New Hope, Pennsylvania, where the writer had just completed his new magnum opus *The Disenchanted*, a novel based on his father and F. Scott Fitzgerald's relationship in Hollywood. At the time, the mighty B. P. Schulberg was reduced to living in his son's guesthouse and taking out employment ads in Hollywood newspapers, thanks to his ruinous addictions to gambling, boozing, and profligate spending and an extramarital affair with movie star Sylvia Sidney that destroyed his marriage and got him squeezed out of his position at Paramount in 1932. Not that living in

New Hope, Pennsylvania, part of Bucks County, was exactly slumming. After all, the brilliant satirist and screenwriter S. J. Perelman lived on an 83-acre farm not all that far from Schulberg's. Fellow neighbors, the married writers Samuel and Bella Spewack, penned such Broadway hits as *Boy Meets Girl* and *Kiss Me Kate* on their Bucks County spread. From his 1840 stone manor house, known as Highland Farm, situated on 40 prime acres of Bucks County real estate, lyricist–librettist Oscar Hammerstein spied cows grazing on a hillside and wrote, "Oh, What a Beautiful Mornin'" for *Oklahoma!* as well as the lyrics for other show-stoppers from *South Pacific*, *The King & I*, and *The Sound of Music*. In and out of Bucks County for weekends in the country were show business royals, including Henry Fonda, Mary Martin, Joshua Logan, James A. Michener, and the young Stephen Sondheim.

Siodmak and Curtis proposed to Schulberg that he use Malcolm Johnson's waterfront reportage as the basis for the project with the chance to work side by side with the director. Deliberately sidestepping executives at Siodmak's home studio Universal to avoid interference on his and Schulberg's work required them to work pretty much on spec. Still, the fiercely independent Schulberg liked the idea and was heartened when Curtis offered to make B. P. Schulberg one of the film's producers. For almost six months, Siodmak and Schulberg worked closely together in New York and digging deep into research, observing and interviewing dockworkers in the wild as their prelude to developing the crime-on-the-waterfront script they provisionally titled "A Stone in the Hudson River." Although organized crime types shadowed and threatened them, the cowriters were excited that they had created something showing great promise. Joseph Curtis proposed that they first put their work in front of Harry Cohn, who rejected it in a demeaning way. More than likely, considering Schulberg's former membership in the Communist Party, Cohn's rejection had more than a tinge of political motivation. On the rebound, Siodmak got Universal interested, but only enough for them to take a modest "courtesy" option. To Hollywood, the project sounded risky and potentially controversial. In time, the bitterly disappointed Siodmak and Schulberg parted on good terms. Siodmak became increasingly weary of Hollywood politics and unsatisfied with such directorial offers as Burt Lancaster's acrobatic, decorative action-adventure picture *The Crimson Pirate*. Before he left the United States in pursuit of what he hoped might be better work abroad, Siodmak channeled a bit of his "A Stone in the Hudson River" research and passion into the unfairly overlooked 1951 movie *The Whistle at Eaton Falls*. Produced on real locations by the enterprising, politically progressive Louis de Rochemont, made in a semi-documentary style and making extensive use of local nonactors to lend a more authentic feel, Siodmak centered his narrative on a union leader and new factory boss (played by Lloyd Bridges) who gets branded as a traitor by anti-union rabble-rousers fomenting labor relations unrest in a New Hampshire factory town.

## Miller Time

Curtis and Siodmak moved on. Enter playwright Arthur Miller, who was about to play a highly significant role in the *Waterfront* saga. In 1944, at age 29, Miller had endured one humiliating Broadway flop with his *The Man Who Had All the Luck*. A parable about a young, self-taught mechanic who somehow sails above everyone else's utter catastrophes, it closed after four performances. Miller, disheartened and ready to "find another line of work," undertook his next play as a do-or-die enterprise. *All My Sons*, directed by Elia Kazan, opened at the Coronet Theater (known later as the Eugene O'Neill Theater) in January 1947 and dissected the moral reckoning of a family-oriented factory owner who sells faulty cylinder heads, used in World War II military aircraft engines, that lead to the deaths of several American soldiers. Bristling with criticism of the greed, moral duplicity, and lies Miller found at the heart of the American Dream, the play starred Ed Begley, Karl Malden, and Arthur Kennedy and ran for nearly a year, and the film rights sold to Hollywood. In 1949, Miller became the centerpiece of a more thunderous success with *Death of a Salesman*, again directed by Kazan. Starring Lee J. Cobb, Mildred Dunnock, Arthur Kennedy, Howard Smith, and Cameron Mitchell, it ran for 742 performances at the Morosco Theatre, earned six Tony Awards and became the first play to sweep all three top theatrical awards. Miller won a personal Tony Award, the New York Drama Critics' Circle Award, and the Pulitzer Prize for Drama. With Miller's talents drawing favorable comparisons to those of Strindberg, Ibsen, and O'Neill, *Death of a Salesman* marked a dizzying creative peak for both the playwright and director Kazan. The play remains one of the most celebrated, filmed, and revived works in American theatrical history.

Intent on finding material on which to collaborate again, Miller and Kazan kept each other apprised of their progress on various projects. Kazan had been especially encouraging about Miller's idea to write an original dramatic screenplay set on the Brooklyn waterfront; the writer had roughed out the notion to Kazan when they'd first met in 1946. Miller had watched Kazan filming *Boomerang* (a fact-based movie released in 1947 about a Connecticut vagrant falsely accused of shooting a priest) and mentioned how he was thinking about taking another stab at writing for films. Having been demoralized by getting replaced as screenwriter of the 1945 film *The Story of G.I. Joe*, Miller, two years later, was disappointed at being unable to strike sparks with Alfred Hitchcock, who had offered him the chance to adapt Patrick Hamilton's 1929 play *Rope* for the big screen.

Previous experience made Miller develop an approach-avoidance stance toward Hollywood and its general disregard for serious writers, but he was hardly idle. During this intensely creative period, he worked on his stage adaptation of Henrik Ibsen's *An Enemy of the People*, which opened on Broadway on December 28, 1950. But throughout four months, Miller had continued developing his waterfront screenplay, now titled *The Hook*. In May 1949, Miller finished another draft of *The Hook*. Kazan read it and considered it "a half-assed job," as the script completely failed to fully dramatize the themes and concerns he had set out to tackle. He advised Miller to go back to the source. Miller had spent some of his formative years growing up on the Brooklyn waterfront and realized that one source of his fascination with *The Hook* was the people of dockside Red Hook, a western Brooklyn community on the knife edge of transformation. Another of Miller's inspirations, which as he had begun telling interviewers as early as 1948, was the mysterious 1939 disappearance of Brooklyn dockworker Pietro "Pete" Panto, who had stood up against the mob. While roaming Red Hook during his research forays, Miller repeatedly encountered graffiti chalked on the community's sidewalks and buildings—*Dov'è Pete Panto? Where is Pete Panto?* Panto was a 29-year-old Italian American who had tried to organize his fellow longshoremen to break the stranglehold of the deeply corrupt, mob-infested ILA. For a short time, it looked like he might succeed. At outdoor rallies, which attracted as many as 1,500 dockworkers, the impassioned Panto rabble-roused for the reform of the dangerous working conditions and poor wages workers faced on the Brooklyn docks. He railed against the iron-fisted, all-powerful ILA "lifetime" president, Joseph Ryan ("King Joe" to the workers) for miring that association in Mob control, police complicity, political patronage, and a sweetheart deal with shipowners.

Not surprisingly, the ILA punched back at Panto and his grassroots Brooklyn Rank-and-File Committee by trying to label them as "radicals," "reds," and "commies." But when those labels didn't stick, they instead tried bribing Panto, who refused to stand down. Then Panto received explicit threats from ILA Vice President Emil Camarda, who controlled 4,000 members of various ILA unions from the Brooklyn Bridge all the way to 20th Street. One of Camarda's closest associates was Mafia honcho Vincent Mangano, a head of the Five Families crime syndicate of New York, which exist to the day and include the Bonanno, Colombo, Gambino, Genovese, and Lucchese families. On Bastille Day, July 14, 1939, three members of the Mafia's Murder, Incorporated death squad—Mendy Weiss, Tony Romanello, and James Ferraco—abducted Panto. Allegedly, under orders from Albert Anastasia, head of Brooklyn's ILA Local 1814 and the brother of the capo of what later became known as the Gambino crime family, Mendy Weiss strangled Panto and dumped his body in the lime pit of a Lyndhurst, New Jersey, chicken farm. The message was clear: President Joe Ryan was not to be challenged. To this day, the case remains unsolved. Authorities only discovered Panto's decomposed corpse two years after his murder.

News of Miller's interest in using Panto as an inspiration for *The Hook* drew the attention of several sympathetic figures who offered support and assistance, including local American Labor Party member Mitch Berenson, who doggedly pursued his mission to expose the ILA and its president, Joseph Ryan, for corruption and gangland connections. Additionally, Miller's local guide became attorney Vincent "Jimmy" Longhi, who had been delving deeply into the spread of graft and corruption. Both men helped give Miller what he and Kazan feared the screenplay lacked: an insider's understanding of an insular community's arcane laws of silence and codes of honor. Miller began frequenting Red Hook bars, where he gained the trust of local longshoremen who shared their financial, physical, and existential hardships. He spent many early mornings observing the degrading "shape-up" system of hiring, described in Malcolm Johnson's "Crime on the Waterfront" article as "an archaic and degrading hoax—it leaves the hiring of dockworkers entirely up to the union and opens up the gates wide for every type of racket and malpractice." The morning shape-up saw hundreds of men turn up on the docks at an appointed hour.

Each one was desperate to be chosen for dangerous, low-paying day work by the hiring stevedore, who, wrote Johnson, "possesses the power of economic life or death over them."

Miller feverishly rewrote the new work, which he now titled, variously, *Shape-Up: A Screen Treatment*, and *The Hook: A Play for the Screen*, and finally, back where he began, simply *The Hook*. The title gained new layers of meaning, referencing not only the Red Hook neighborhood setting but also the docker's hook tool used daily by longshoremen. The title also slyly references "Give him the hook!," the command shouted by raucous vaudeville audiences when they disapproved of a stage performance; armed with a long hook attached to a broom, a theater employee would literally yank the poor performers offstage and into the wings, to the audience's cheers and jeers. By any of its titles, Miller's script makes for fascinating reading. He hinges the action on the anguished rage of an Italian American dockworker named "Marty Ferrara" who witnesses the death of a coworker crushed while unloading cargo. Marty and the other men are immediately ordered back to work, and the frantic pace of the dangerous job begins all over again. Outraged by the barbarism of the shape-up, the daily work risks, and the union president selling memberships to the highest bidder, Marty expresses to his wife, in a scene set in a park playground, that he feels their lives should be worth much more but doesn't know how to break the cycle of dock work. He takes a job with a local bookie but quits when overcome by the guilt and shame he feels toward exploiting his destitute fellow working men.

Marty returns to work on the docks and tries to keep his head down, but the dam breaks when, discovering that many of his fellow workers are being denied overtime pay, he attempts to organize them into a work stoppage. He urges, "Just stand up for yourselfs, that's all! Be human bein's for five minutes." No one backs him up. But that same night, Marty—in a scene that echoes *An Enemy of the*

*People*—makes a speech at the union hall and throws away his union workbook, saying: "These finks, they scared of us. The kids used to say, 'Go down to the piers and you'll see the real big rats. The tough guys.' I've never seen no big rats on the waterfront. I only found little scared rats. I've seen rats kicked around on the ships, killed on the ships. Only tonight, we got big rats in the house tonight. If these finks can take from me my bread and butter, then I'm a slave in a chain. I was born in Italy but this—this is fascism."

For speaking inconvenient truths, Marty's life swirls down the drain. Miller goes heavy on the misery and martyrdom. Marty gets suspended by the union, becomes persona non grata; the power company shuts off his electricity for nonpayment; his furniture gets repossessed; and he's reduced to stealing spare change from rummies to buy himself jugs of rotgut. He pulls himself together long enough to challenge Louis for the union presidency and gives a fiery speech that draws cheers from the longshoremen. Despite massive voter turnout, Marty loses the election. The beaten-down workers vote against their own self-interest. Marty gets bought off with a token union delegate position, but during the shape-up, he cries out to his coworkers, "Don't dive for this! You ain't no cattle!" The longshoremen erupt in a confused, joyful, angry riot, finally inspired to action by a union rep who can't be bought off. The finale is rousing but painfully naïve, and Kazan, though unconvinced, urged Miller to dig deeper on the next rewrite.

The more Miller worked on the screenplay, the more attracted he was by the thematic resonance of the charismatic Peter Panto's crusade than to the biographical details of his life or death. Miller spoke of Panto as a man brave enough to stand up to waterfront thuggery for the benefit of longshoremen and their families living under a "reign of quiet terror." On completing what he felt was a stronger draft of *The Hook* in May 1949, the writer spoke to a *New York Herald-Tribune* journalist about what he called his "play written for the screen by Arthur Miller" and announced that it would be filmed locally by Elia Kazan and produced *independently* by Kazan and Broadway stage producer Kermit Bloomgarden (*Death of a Salesman*). Translation? Kazan anticipated what a hard sell to mainstream Hollywood the project would be. The Bloomgarden office prepared the contracts. Kazan never signed them. Perhaps because by 1950, Kazan's career had hit a whole new level: he had just finished making *Panic in the Streets*, the manhunt melodrama shot on the streets of New Orleans, as part of his rich, nonexclusive six-movie deal with 20th Century Fox's boss Darryl F. Zanuck. Being offered virtually every new play and film project and set to begin filming *A Streetcar Named Desire* for Warner Bros., Kazan decided on doing *The Hook* next but not as an independent production. Now he wanted to show Hollywood that he could make an uncompromising, powerful film worthy of his reputation as an artist—but he wanted to make it with all the heft and access a big studio could afford him: a handpicked cast, a decent budget, showy advertising, and an awards consideration publicity campaign. Meanwhile, he urged Miller to take another crack at rewriting *The Hook*.

Miller might well have wondered whether Kazan was stringing him along. After all, the director's focus seemed divided. In January 1951, after a Santa Monica, California, sneak preview screening of *A Streetcar Named Desire* had sparked unwanted laughs, Kazan went rushing back into the editing bay. Meanwhile, he and his screenwriter, John Steinbeck, were deep into preproduction on a film to star Marlon Brando as Emiliano Zapata, the Mexican revolutionary with whom Kazan had been fascinated since the 1930s. Somehow, Zanuck seemed to envision the project as a jumped-up, classy Western, and to keep things rolling along, neither Kazan nor Steinbeck bothered to disabuse him of the notion.

Also in January, Miller and Kazan rode west from Grand Central Station to Los Angeles aboard the 20th Century Limited and the Santa Fe Super Chief with the objective of finding movie studio financing for *The Hook*. En route, Kazan shared his plan to shoot the movie in a gritty Italian neorealist style, the better to emphasize the extreme hardships and perils faced by the proles on the docks. Miller's biographer, Martin Gottfried, asserts another agenda on the part of the "manipulative director." The satyr Kazan was convinced that young Miller was "starved for sexual release" and his work was showing it. He intended to plunge the writer into a Hollywood Babylon-style playland. Their base of operations was to be the lavish Coldwater Canyon home of married playboy and bon vivant Charles K. Feldman, legendary cocksman and party-giver, budding major film producer of Kazan's film of *Streetcar*, and the talent agent whose triple-A client list included the starry likes of Humphrey Bogart, Marlene Dietrich, Howard Hawks, Greta Garbo, Claudette Colbert, John Wayne, Lauren Bacall, and Susan Hayward.

The Feldman house was built in 1935 in the Spanish Colonial style and given a Hollywood Regency–style facelift by William Haines, movie star turned makeover interior designer, in 1942. In the hands of Feldman and his glamorous photographer-hostess former wife, Jean Howard, the house was a mecca of high-minded evenings hosting their friends Noël Coward, Irving Berlin, Jean Cocteau, and Cole Porter as well as evenings of unbridled ha-cha. Even when the gregarious Feldman was out of town, he allowed the soirées to continue, populated by young stunners, many of them starlets, who floated in and out. The revelers also numbered well-connected, middle-aged men with access and power unmatched by that of the young women. Among them was the striking 25-year-old, anatomically astonishing blonde starlet Marilyn Monroe.

Monroe had been knocking around town for the past six years. Despite having in her corner (and in her bed) a powerful William Morris Office agent named Johnny Hyde and, later, Feldman himself, Monroe had yet to make a real dent on-screen outside of small roles Hyde had scrounged for his protégée in *The Asphalt Jungle* and *All About Eve*. There was a 31-year age difference between them, yet the ungainly, diminutive 55-year-old Hyde (as Monroe's "Miss Caswell" laments in *All About Eve*, "Why do they always look like unhappy rabbits?") had left his wife and repeatedly asked Monroe to marry him as often as she refused. Shortly after he landed Monroe a contract with 20th Century Fox, Hyde died unexpectedly in December 1950. The loss of her friend and protector left Monroe bereft. Elia Kazan, whose agent was Hyde's boss Abe Lastfogel, knew of Monroe's deep insecurities and psychological disarray, her history of being shuttled from foster home to foster home, the abuse she suffered, and her ceaseless search for validation. He even wrote to his wife about Monroe, calling her "talented, funny, vulnerable, helpless in awful pain" and comparing the hardships of her past to those of every Charlie Chaplin heroine combined. Her role in the lives of Kazan and Miller and in *On the Waterfront* was about to happen.

Once Kazan and Miller settled into their chez Feldman digs, they and Abe Lastfogel made their first stop at the offices of Darryl Zanuck at 20th Century Fox. Uppermost in the mind of the chief of Kazan's "home studio" wasn't *The Hook*, though, but how soon Kazan and Steinbeck would deliver the final script for *Viva Zapata!* The fortunes of that project hinged on snagging the red hot, mercurial Marlon Brando, who'd been turning down big projects with impunity. Lastfogel and Kazan assured (or, rather, bluffed) the studio chief that the Mexican revolutionary script was on track and steered the conversation back to *The Hook*. Zanuck wanted to stay in business with the hottest director on both coasts, but he had already read Miller's script and didn't like its chances, saying, "It's exactly what audiences don't want to see now." Kazan gave up on Zanuck in the face of such obstinacy but resented Lastfogel's caving in without fighting for him. In truth, the rejection disheartened Miller and Kazan rather than surprised them. Next on Lastfogel's list was a solo meeting with Jack Warner, who was bullish on the prospects of *A Streetcar Named Desire*, his studio's first movie from Kazan soon to open in New York. Although Warner wanted to lure Kazan from Zanuck and Fox, he, too, was cold on *The Hook*. So were the bosses of MGM, Paramount, and Universal.

While Miller and Kazan waited for word from Lastfogel on their next moves, they lingered on the Fox lot. Can it possibly be accidental that Kazan suggested they visit the set of *As Young as You Feel*, a Monty Wooley–Thelma Ritter comedy in which Marilyn Monroe was playing the small role of a secretary? Kazan and Miller arrived just in time to witness first-time director Harmon Jones (Kazan's editor on *Gentleman's Agreement*, *Pinky*, and *Panic in the Streets*) badger and demean Monroe to the point of her fleeing the set in tears. Kazan followed her and found her weeping in the corner of a nearby dark and empty soundstage. She struck him as unschooled but intelligent, vulnerable, a deep well of raw emotion. He consoled her, walked her back to the set, and introduced her to Miller, who apparently looked like he'd been struck by lightning.

With Charles Feldman away for several days, Kazan prodded Miller to spend his daylight hours working at a typewriter on a poolside table and making something more sinewy and vital of *The Hook*, which he faulted for being a verbose and preachy screenplay. By night, Kazan and Marilyn Monroe entertained themselves in a nearby bedroom while Miller continued to clack away at the typewriter. But Monroe, Miller admitted, was a creature he "desperately wanted," and soon he would get her. Feldman returned from his travels with Jean Howard, with whom he had remained intimate despite their 1948 divorce, and both were so taken by Miller that they chose to make him the guest of honor at a lavish Friday-night party on January 26, 1951, replete with a full orchestra and guest list that included Humphrey Bogart and Lauren Bacall, actress Evelyn Keyes (who had recently shed her film director–writer husband,

John Huston), directors William Wyler and Charles Chaplin, and others. Also on the Feldmans' guest list was written "Kazan's date" (a nameless Monroe). But at the last minute, Kazan gave Monroe's phone number to Miller and asked him to take her to the party since he would be occupied until late on some pressing casting matters for *Viva Zapata!* Kazan was reportedly occupied with Monroe's stunning friend, *As Young as You Feel* costar Jean Peters, whom he had also chatted up on the set. A highly intelligent, gifted protégée of Howard Hughes (whom she married in 1957), Peters won the role in *Viva Zapata!*

Meanwhile, from the moment Miller and Monroe entered the room—the carnal, glittering, misunderstood Hollywood creation decorating the arm of the Pulitzer Prize–winning New York intellectual and theatrical wizard—they became the talk of the party. They danced like they were molded together. They canoodled on the sofa while Miller caressed Monroe's shoeless foot. Miller listened to her more than he spoke, which was something entirely new. They looked "totally wrapped up" in each other, according to one guest. By the time Kazan arrived, even the self-absorbed director could see how Monroe blossomed in Miller's company. So it was Miller, not Kazan, who saw Marilyn home after the party. But it was Kazan who later churlishly asked how things had gone with Miller. Monroe guilelessly offered, "He was shy." Kazan gloated.

For a time in Hollywood, Miller and Kazan became Marilyn's *Jules and Jim.* If she was not Kazan's Catherine, she certainly became Miller's. They'd dine out as a convivial threesome. They'd shop at Hollywood bookstores, and Miller would recommend poets to her (Walt Whitman, e.e. cummings, Robert Frost) and autographed the copy she bought of *Death of a Salesman.* Kazan convinced Miller that they should have Monroe (wearing an owlish pair of prop glasses and carrying a steno pad) pose as Kazan's temporary secretary "Miss Bauer" at a meeting about *The Hook* with Harry Cohn, the notoriously tightfisted, vulgar head of production at Columbia Pictures. In those days, in status-obsessed Hollywood, Columbia was a far cry from the prestigious 20th Century Fox, MGM, or Warner Bros. Even its headquarters squatted on the unprepossessing corner of Sunset and Gower, an area nicknamed "Gower Gulch" since 1940 when the manager of the local Columbia Drugs allowed real cowboys to use the pay phone to call Central Casting when they were scrounging for movie gigs.

\* \* \*

Cohn was a maverick, bully, inveterate meddler, and fire-breather, but Kazan knew how to push back. Nicknamed "White Fang" by screenwriter-playwright Ben Hecht, Cohn respected countervailing forces—especially since he so rarely encountered them. He said of himself in 1946, "I may be known as a crude, loudmouth son-of-a-bitch, but I built Columbia. I started it with spit and wire and these fists. I stole, cheated, and beat people's brains out. Columbia is not just my love; it's my baby, my life. I'd die without Columbia." Cohn, who also had an eye for beauty, asked several times during the meeting whether he and the comely "Miss Bauer" had met previously. But he remained clueless about her actual identity. Besides, for once, the man whose sexual advances were repelled by Joan Crawford, Ginger Rogers, Rita Hayworth, and others had more pressing matters on his mind. Although not especially excited about *The Hook*, he saw the upside of establishing an ongoing relationship with the prestigious Kazan and Miller. Columbia was, after all, distributing the Stanley Kramer–produced screen version of Miller's *Death of a Salesman*.

As for Miller, when he wasn't gazing at Monroe studiously scribbling notes in her steno pad, he believed that the meeting was going their way. After all, wasn't Cohn making noises about budgets, casting, rehearsal dates, and shooting schedules? If Miller had been listening more closely, he would have heard Cohn telling them that any up-front money would be meager and if *The Hook* got made at all, it would be on a shoestring budget. Still, the men made a tentative verbal commitment, and Cohn set a date for a second meeting. Meanwhile, the inside moves began. With the rise of anti-Communism mania in the United States, Cohn developed a case of cold feet over Miller and Kazan's portrayal of a union and an organized labor force thumbscrewed by corruption and gang rule. To hedge his bets, he had *The Hook* script vetted by shrewd, tough-minded arch conservative Roy Brewer, president of both the powerful union of the International Alliance of Theatrical Stage Employees and the anti-communist Motion Picture Industry Council. The red-baiting Brewer didn't mince words: "The great problem in the unions is the Communist. The racketeers are much less a menace to labor than the Communists." Some controversy surrounds the second meeting with Cohn and Brewer. Miller, in his autobiographical book, *Timebends*, wrote that he had already departed the West Coast for New York when the meeting took place and that Kazan phoned to fill him in on the details. But Kazan and Brewer both documented that Miller was present. Either way, according to Miller, Brewer proposed major changes to the screenplay, the biggest of which was that Communists, not racketeers, would be the heavies. But Kazan and Brewer both insisted that Communism only be suggested as subtext. The subject surfaced in a 1990 phone conversation I had with Miller when he was promoting the release of *Everybody Wins*, a Karel Reisz–directed, Miller-scripted thriller movie starring Debra Winger and Nick Nolte based on Miller's 1984 one-act play *Some Kind of Love Story*. When I asked about *The Hook*, Miller asserted, "They expected me to turn the villains of the script into Communists. I refused." Brewer also proposed that the movie open with a foreword about the threat to unions posed by the Red Menace. Kazan feigned agreement but only to keep the project in spin. Brewer also floated the idea of Miller's including a scene depicting the idealistic main character rebuffing a *Daily Worker* reporter's offers of help.

In the aftermath of the post–World War II Red Scare, promulgated by the House Un-American Activities Committee used by opportunistic and fearmongering Senator Joseph McCarthy to weed out suspected communists and fellow travelers and subject them to public shaming, anything that could threaten a film's release to theaters—such as, say, the participation of a screenwriter with actual communist sympathies—might send Harry Cohn running for cover. But only a paranoid or zealot could misread Miller's screenplay as pro-communist. Anti-gangster and pro the common man? Sure, but no more than one of Frank Capra's Columbia movies of the 1940s. Empathic and righteous? No doubt. But perhaps in the grip of the hysteria of anti-Communism that possessed the country at the time, that was all that was needed to stir up Brewer. The meeting ended with Cohn wanting Brewer's blessing on *The Hook*. Brewer said that first he wanted to discuss the script with the leaders of the American Federation of Labor, concluding cryptically, "If you plan to make the picture, make it." Brewer left the implied threat hanging in the air. He held the power to publicly vilify the movie, engineer a boycott, and—more dangerously—expose Arthur Miller's Communist sympathies and connections. He mentioned the potential of projectionists refusing to show the film. Said Kazan, "It was a dreadful scene. A man we'd never met, who had nothing to do with the artistic values of our script, seemed to believe he had the power to decide whether or not we could go ahead with the film. We felt humiliated, so much so that we couldn't discuss the problem. We told our secretary, Miss Bauer, only the basic facts." Days after the meeting, Miller complied by sending Kazan new script pages with a note saying that he would write further pages to speak to issues raised by Brewer. But soon after, Miller called Kazan to tell him that he was pulling the script entirely, apparently without providing Kazan with a full explanation.

Why? Someone had tipped off the government about *The Hook*, and official investigations of Miller's and Kazan's political beliefs and past affiliations with the Communist Party were under way. Miller would later write in his autobiography, *Timebends*: "I knew for a fact that there were next to no Communists on the Brooklyn waterfront, so to depict the rank and file in revolt against communism [as Brewer had 'suggested'] rather than racketeers was simply idiotic and I would be ashamed to go near the waterfront again." Miller refused to make the compromise and pulled the script. When Cohn convened a final meeting with Kazan, the studio executive told the director that he was now sure that Miller was a Communist. Wasn't Miller pulling out of the project so he could avoid having to answer any more questions? And Brewer thwarted Miller because *The Hook* could no longer convey the pro-Communist messages Miller wanted to imbed in it? Cohn told Kazan, "I could tell just by looking at him, he's still one of them." And when Kazan asked what Cohn thought of his own political affiliations, the mogul said, "You're just a good-hearted whore like me. We'll find something else to do together." The telegram Cohn fired off to Miller read: "It's interesting how the minute we try to make the script pro-American, you pull out."

On April 9, 1952, Elia Kazan testified before the House Un-American Activities Committee. He assured friends and colleagues that he would not name names but reversed his position, naming eight people he asserted were once members of the Communist Party.

This is the transcript of the statement of Elia Kazan:

(New York City, N.Y., April 9, 1952)
The House Committee on Un-American Activities,
Washington, D.C.
Gentlemen:

I wish to amend the testimony which I gave before you on January 14 of this year, by adding to it this letter and the accompanying sworn affidavit.

In the affidavit I answer the only question which I failed to answer at the hearing, namely, what people I knew to be members of the Communist Party between the summer of 1934, when I joined it, and the late winter or early spring of 1936, when I severed all connection with it.

I have come to the conclusion that I did wrong to withhold these names before, because secrecy serves the Communists, and is exactly what they want. The American people need the facts and all the facts about all aspects of Communism in order to deal with it wisely and effectively. It is my obligation as a citizen to tell everything that I know.

Although I answered all other questions which were put to me before, the naming of these people makes it possible for me to volunteer a detailed description of my own activities and of the general activity which I witnessed. I have attempted to set these down as carefully and fully as my memory allows. In doing so, I have necessarily repeated portions of my former testimony, but I believe that by so doing I have made a more complete picture than if I omitted it.

In the second section of the affidavit, I have tried to review comprehensively my very slight political activity in the 16 years since I left the party. Here again, I have of necessity repeated former testimony, but I wanted to make as complete an over-all picture as my fallible memory allows.

In the third section is a list of the motion pictures I have made and the plays I have chosen to direct. I call your attention to these for they constitute the entire history of my professional activity as a director.

Respectfully,

Elia Kazan

State of New York,

County of New York, ss:

I, Elia Kazan, being duly sworn, depose and say:

I repeat my testimony of January 14, 1952, before the House Committee on Un-American Activities, to the effect that I was a member of the Communist Party from sometime in the summer of 1934 until the late winter or early spring of 1936, when I severed all connection with it permanently.

I want to reiterate that in those years, to my eyes, there was no clear opposition of national interests between the United States and Russia. It was not even clear to me that the American Communist Party was taking its orders from the Kremlin and acting as a Russian agency in this country. On the contrary, it seemed to me at that time that the Party had at heart the cause of the poor and unemployed people whom I saw on the streets about me. I felt that by joining, I was going to help them, I was going to fight Hitler, and strange as it seems today, I felt that I was acting for the good of the American people.

For approximately 19 months of my membership, I was assigned to a "unit" composed of those party members who were, like myself, members of the Group Theater acting company. These were –

Lewis Leverett, co-leader of the unit.

J. Edward Bromber, co-leader of the unit, deceased.

Phoebe Brand (later Mrs. Morris Carnovsky). I was instrumental in bringing her into the Party.

Morris Carnovsky.

Tony Kraber: Along with Wellman (see below), he recruited me into the Party

Paula Miller (later Mrs. Lee Strasberg): We are friends today. I believe that, as she has told me, she quit the Communists long ago. She is far too sensible and balanced a woman, and she is married to too fine and intelligent a man, to have remained among them.

Clifford Odets: He has assured me that he got out about the time I did.

Art Smith.

These are the only members of the unit whom I recall and I believe this to be a complete list. Even at this date I do not believe it would be possible for me to forget anyone.

I believe that in my previous testimony I mentioned that there were nine members in the unit. I was including Michael Gordon, but in searching my recollection I find that I do not recall his having attended any meeting with me.

As I testified previously, two Party functionaries were assigned to "hand the party line" to us new recruits. They were –

V.J. Jerome, who had some sort of official "cultural" commissar position at Party headquarters; and

Andrew Overgaard, a Scandinavian, who was head, as I recall, of the Trader Union Unity League.

There was a third-party official who concerned himself with us, although whether he was officially assigned or merely hung about the theater when he was in New York, I never knew. He told us that he was state organizer for the Party in Tennessee. He was obviously stagestruck and he undertook to advise me. He was –

Ted Wellman, also known as Sid Benson.

Our financial contributions and dues were on a puny scale. We were small-salaried actors, frequently out of work, and it was depression time.

What we were asked to do was fourfold:

1. To "educate" ourselves in Marxist and Party doctrine;
2. To help the party get a foothold in the Actors Equity Association;
3. To support various "front" organizations of the Party;
4. To try to capture the Group Theater and make it a Communist mouthpiece.

The history of these efforts in my time, were as follows:

In the "education" program we were sold pamphlets and books and told to read them. There were also "discussions" of these. The "discussions" were my first taste of totalitarian methods, for there was no honest discussion at all, but only an attempt to make sure that we swallowed every sentence without challenge.

1. The attempt to gain a foothold in Actors Equity was guided by an actor, Robert or Bob Gaille (I think that was the spelling). He was also known as Bob Reed. I have been told that he died some years ago.

The tactic—and the sincere effort of many individuals—was to "raise a demand" that actors receive pay during the weeks when they rehearsed for shows. The long-range plan was, by leading a fight for a reasonable gain for the actors, to gain prestige for individual Communists and sympathizers who, the party hoped, would then run the union.

Pay for the rehearsal period was obtained, but at no time that I saw either then or after I left, did the Party come within sight of controlling the actors' union.

2. Most of our time, however, went directly or indirectly into providing "entertainment" for the meetings and rallies of front organizations and unions. The "entertainment" was strictly propaganda.

There were two front organizations in the theater field, but off Broadway, whose purpose was to provide such propaganda entertainment and with whom I had dealings. They were the League of Workers Theaters (later the New Theater League) and the Theater of Action. It was into these that my time went. I acted, I trained and directed other actors and, with Art Smith, I co-authored a play called Dimitroff, which had to do with the imprisonment of the Bulgarian Communist leader by the Nazis following the Reichstag fire. It is my memory that the play enjoyed either two or three Sunday night performances before benefit audiences and was then retired.

I taught at the school for actors and directors run by the League of Workers Theaters. This was unquestionably a Communist-controlled outfit. Its officials were never bona fide theater people and it was my impression that they had been imported by the Party from other fields to regiment the political novices in the theater. To the best of my knowledge, when he [sic] league came to an end, they retired from the theater again. I do not recall any Communist meeting which I attended with them, but my impression that they were all Communists is very strong. The ones I remember were –

1. Harry Elion, president.
2. John Bonn, a German refugee.
3. Alice Evans (I am told she later married V.J. Jerome)
4. Anne Howe.

In the Theater of Action, there was a Communist thought and behavior and control, but I did not attend their political meetings so I cannot tell which of the actors were Party members and which were not. I did some acting training here and I co-directed with Al Saxe a play called *The Young Go First*, and I directed another called (I think) *The Crisis*.

About 1936, I began a connection with an outfit called Frontier Films, but the Party had nothing to do with my making this connection. The organization consisted of four or five men, of whom I remember Paul Strand, Leo Hurwitz, and Ralph Steiner. From long friendship with Steiner, I believe him to be a strong anti-Communist. I do not know the Party affiliation of the others. They were trying to raise money to make documentary films. They put me on their board, but I attended few meetings. I wanted to make a picture. This I did, with Ralph Steiner, in 1937. It was a two-reel documentary called *The People of the Cumberlands*.

That was my last active connection with any organization which has since been listed as subversive.

3. I want to repeat emphatically that the Communists' attempt to take over the Group Theater failed. There was some influence and a great deal of talk, the members of the Communist unit consumed a great deal of time at group meetings, they raised some money from the non-Communist members for Communists' causes and they sold them some Communist pamphlets; they brought the prestige of the group name to meetings where they entertained as individuals, but they never succeeded in controlling the Group Theater.

This was because the control of the group stayed firmly in the hands of the three non-Communist directors, Harold Clurman, Lee Strasberg, and Cheryl Crawford. (In 1937 Clurman became sole director and remained so until the theater broke up in 1940.)

In a small way, I played a part in blocking the Communist unit's maneuvers to get control. In the winter of 1935–1936, I was a member of the actors' committee of the group. This was an advisory committee, but it was the nearest the actors ever came to having any voice in the running of the theater. I was instructed by the Communist unit to demand that the group be run "democratically." This was a characteristic Communist tactic; they were not interested in democracy; they wanted control. They had no chance of controlling the directors, but they thought that if authority went to the actors, they would have a chance to dominate through the usual tricks of behind-the-scenes caucuses, block voting, and confusion of issues.

This was the specific issue on which I quit the party. I had enough of their habitual violation of the daily practices of democracy to which I was accustomed. The last straw came when I was invited to go through a typical Communist scene of crawling and apologizing and admitting the error of my ways. The invitation came from a Communist functionary brought in for the occasion. He was introduced as an organizer of the Auto

Workers Union from Detroit. I regret that I cannot remember his name. In any case, he probably did not use his own name. I had never seen him before, nor he me.

He made a vituperative analysis of my conduct in refusing to fall in with the Party line and plan for the Group Theater, and he invited my repentance. My fellow members looked at him as if he were an oracle. I have not seen him since, either.

That was the night I quit them. I had had enough anyway. I had had a taste of police-state living and I did not like it. Instead of working honestly for the good of the American people, I had found that I was being used to put power in the hands of people for whom, individually and as a group, I felt nothing but contempt, and for whose standard of conduct I felt a genuine horror.

Since that night, I have never had the least thing to do with the Party.

After I left the Party in 1936, except for the making of the two-reel documentary film mentioned above, in 1937, I was never active in any organization since listed as subversive.

My policy in the years after 1936 was an instinctive rather than a planned one. I could usually detect a front organization when I first heard about it and I stayed away from it. I never became a member of such an organization, although I was pressed to join dozens of them.

Contradictorily, on a few of the many occasions when I was asked to sign a statement or a telegram for a specific cause, I may have allowed my name to be used, even though I suspected the sponsoring organization. The insidiously picked causes which appealed to decent, liberal, humanitarian people; against racial discrimination, against Japanese aggression, against specific miscarriages of justice. There was a piece of spurious reasoning which influenced me to let them use my name in rare instances. It went like this, "I hate Communists but I go along with this cause because I believe the cause is right."

Today I repudiate that reasoning, but it accounts for those of the instances listed below in which I may have done what is alleged. I repudiate the reasoning because I believe that all their fights are deceitful maneuvers to gain influence.

My connections with these front organizations were so slight and so transitory that I am forced to rely on a listing of these prepared for me after research by my employer, 20th Century Fox. I state with full awareness that I am under oath, that in most of the cases I do not remember any connection at all. It is possible that my name was used without my consent. It is possible that in a few instances I gave consent.

I am told that the *New Masses* of November 4, and the *Daily Worker* of November 8, 1941, list me as an entertainer at a meeting sponsored by the American Friends of the Chinese People. I remember no connection whatsoever with this organization and especially since I ceased all "entertaining" in 1936 when I left the Party, I can only suppose that my name was used without my permission in this instance.

I am told that I signed an appeal put out by the Committee for a Boycott Against Japanese Aggression. I do not remember this either, but it is possible that I signed such an appeal. No date is given but it must have been before Pearl Harbor.

I am told that the official program of the Artists Front To Win the War listed me as a sponsor in October 1942. I have no memory of this either but it is possible that I gave my consent to the use of my name.

I am told that on July 19, 1942, I signed an open letter sponsored by the National Federation for Constitutional Liberties, which denounced Attorney General [Francis] Biddle's charges against [the International Longshoremen's Association union leader] Harry Bridges. I have no recollection of this either, but again it is possible that I did so, for I remember that, in contrast to what I had heard about the New York waterfront, what I had heard about San Francisco suggested that Bridges had done a good job for his union. And I remember that I believed the story, current at that time, that he was being hounded for this. At that time I did not believe him to be a Communist.

I have been reminded that my name was used as a sponsor of the publication, *People's Songs*. I have no doubt that I gave permission for this. The date could be found by referring to the first issues of the publication. Beyond allowing my name to be used initially, I had no contact with it.

The only money contribution which I remember between 1936 and 1947 or 1948—and I remember it with regret—was one of $200 which I gave to Arnaud d'Usseau when he asked for help in founding what he said was to be a new "liberal literary magazine." This magazine turned out to be *Mainstream* and from its first issue was a patently Communist publication altogether detestable and neither liberal nor literary.

Now I come to the only case or cause in which I got involved, even to a limited extent, in those sixteen years between 1936 and 1952. It was what became known as the case of the Hollywood Ten.

I would recall to this Committee the opening of the first investigation into Communism in Hollywood by the previous committee under the chairmanship of J. Parnell Thomas. I would recall that a large number of representative people in the creative branch of the picture industry, regardless of their politics, were alarmed by the first sessions. They signed protests and they banded in organizations which certainly did not look to me like front organizations at their inception, although later the Communists plainly got control of them.

I am listed as sponsoring a committee to raise funds for the defense of the Ten and as having sent a telegram to John Huston on March 5, 1948, when he was chairman of the dinner for them. I do not remember these specific actions, but I certainly felt impelled to action of that sort at that time and did this or something like it. I also made a contribution of $500 to a woman representative of the committee for the Hollywood Ten. This was in New York. If I am able to recall her name, I will advise you of it, but I cannot recall it at the moment. I am also listed as supporting a radio program for the Ten as late as August 1950. I am surprised at the date. It is possible that I was approached and gave permission to use my name as late as this, but it seems to me more likely that my name was reused without asking me, since I had not allowed its use earlier.

For by that time I was disgusted by the silence of the Ten and by their contemptuous attitude. However, I must say now that what I did earlier represented my convictions at the beginning of the case.

That is the end of the list of my front associations after 1936, insofar as I can remember them, with the assistance of the memorandum prepared for me.

I should like to point out some of the typical Communist-front and Communist-sympathizer activities which I stayed away from:

From the day I went to Hollywood to direct my first picture, in 1944, I had nothing to do with any front organization there. Neither had I anything to do with them on three earlier trips as an actor. I had nothing to do with the Actor's Lab. I never gave a penny to any front organization on the West Coast.

I did not sign the Stockholm peace pledge. I saw what that was. I resented the Communist attempt to capture the world "peace."

I did not sponsor or attend the Waldorf Peace Conference. My wife's name was used as a sponsor without her permission. She protested and asked for its withdrawal in a letter to Prof. Harlow Shapley of Harvard University, who had some official post. She received no answer from him, but she did get an apology from James Proctor, who had given her name without permission.

I had nothing to do with the Arts, Sciences, and Professions or any of its predecessors or successors.

I did not support Henry Wallace for President.

I do not want to imply that anyone who did these things was one of the Communists; I do not submit that anyone who did none of them was a long way away from them.

III

There follows a list of my entire professional career as a director, all the plays I have done and films I have made.

*Casey Jones*, by Robert Audrey, 1938: The story of a railroad engineer who comes to the end of his working days. It is thoroughly and wonderfully American in its tone, characters, and outlook.

*Thunder Rock*, by Robert Ardry, 1939: This is a deeply democratic and deeply optimistic play, written at a time when there was a good deal of pessimism about democracy. It told of a group of European immigrants headed for the West about 1848, and showed how they despaired of reforms which this country had long since achieved and now takes for granted. A failure in New York, this play was a huge hit in wartime London.

*Café Crown*, by Hy Kraft, 1942: A comedy about Jewish actors on New York's East Side. No politics, but a warm and friendly feeling toward a minority of a minority.

*The Strings, My Lord, Are False*, by Paul Vincent Carroll, 1942: An Irishman's play about England under the bombings. Not political. It shows human courage and endurance in many kinds of people, including, prominently, a priest.

*The Skin of Our Teeth*, by Thornton Wilder, 1942: One of the plays I am proudest to have done. It celebrates the endurance of the human race and does so with wit and wisdom and compassion.

*Harriet*, by Florence Ryerson and Colin Clements, 1943: The story of Harriet Beecher Stowe, who wrote *Uncle Tom's Cabin*.

*One Touch of Venus*, by S.J. Perelman, Ogden Nash, and Kurt Weill, 1943: Musical comedy. The goddess of Venus falls in love with a barber.

*Jacobowsky and the Colonel*, by S.N. Behrman, 1942: Humorous-sad tale of the flight of a Jewish jack-of-all-trades and a Polish count before the oncoming Nazis. Not political, but very human.

*A Tree Grows in Brooklyn* (my first picture), 1944: A little girl grows up in the slum section of Brooklyn. There is pain in the story, but there is health. It is a typically American story and could only happen here, and a glorification of America not in material terms, but in spiritual ones.

*Sing Out Sweet Land*, by Jean and Walter Kerr, 1944: A musical built around old American songs. Nonpolitical but full of American tradition and spirit.

*Deep Are the Roots*, by Arnaud d'Usseau and James Gow, 1945: This was a very frank and somewhat melodramatic exploration of relations between Negroes and whites. It was shocking to some people but on the whole both audiences and critics took it with enthusiasm.

*Dunnigan's Daughter*, by S.N. Behrman, 1945: A comedy drama about a young wife whose husband was too absorbed in his business to love her.

*Sea of Grass* (picture), 1946: The conflict between cattle ranchers and farmers on the prairie.

*Boomerang* (picture), 1946: Based on an incident in the life of Homer Cummings, later Attorney General of the United States. It tells how an initial miscarriage of justice was righted by the persistence and integrity of a young district attorney, who risked his career to save an innocent man. This shows the exact opposite of the Communist libels on America.

*All My Sons*, by Arthur Miller, 1947: The story of a war veteran who came home to discover that his father, a small manufacturer, had shipped defective plane parts to the Armed Forces during the war. Some people have searched for hidden propaganda in this one, but I believe it to be a deeply moral investigation of problems of conscience and responsibility.

*Gentleman's Agreement* (picture): Picture version of the best-selling novel about anti-Semitism. It won an academy award and I think it is in a healthy American tradition, for it shows Americans exploring a problem and tackling a solution. Again it is opposite to the picture which Communists present of Americans.

*A Streetcar Named Desire*, by Tennessee Williams, 1947: A famous play. Not political, but deeply human.

*Sundown Beach*, by Bessie Breuer, 1948: A group of young Army fliers and their girls at a hospital in Florida. Not political, but a warm and compassionate treatment.

*Lovelife*, by Alan Jay Lerner and Kurt Weill, 1948: Musical comedy. Story of a married couple, covering 100 years of changing American standards and customs.

*Death of a Salesman*, by Arthur Miller, 1949: It shows the frustrations of the life of a salesman and contains implicit criticism of his materialistic standards.

*Pinky* (picture), 1949: The story of a Negro girl who passed for white in the North and returns to the South to encounter freshly the impact of prejudice. Almost everybody liked this except the Communists, who attacked it virulently. It was extremely successful throughout the country, as much so in the South as elsewhere.

*Panic in the Streets* (picture), 1950: A melodrama built around the subject of an incipient plague. The hero is a doctor in the United States Health Service.

*A Streetcar Named Desire* (picture), 1950: Picture version of the play.

*Viva Zapata!* (picture, my most recent one), 1951: This is an anti-Communist picture. Please see my article on political aspects of this picture in the *Saturday Review* of April 5, which I forwarded to your investigator, Mr. Nixon.

*Flight Into Egypt*, by George Tabori, 1952: Story of refugees stranded in Cairo and trying to get into the United States.

I think it is useful that certain of us had this kind of experience with the Communists, for if we had not, we should not know them so well. Anyone who has had it is not to be fooled by them again. Today, when all the world fears war and they scream peace, we know how much their professions are worth. We know tomorrow they will have a new slogan.

Firsthand experience of the dictatorship and thought control left me with an abiding hatred of these. It left me with an abiding hatred of Communist philosophy and methods.

It also left me with the passionate conviction that we must never let the Communists get away with the pretense that they stand for the very things which they kill in their own countries.

I am talking about free speech, a free press, the rights of labor, racial equality and, above all, individual rights. I value these things. I take them seriously. I value peace, too, when it is not bought at the price of fundamental decencies.

I believe these things must be fought for wherever they are not fully honored and protected whenever they are threatened.

The motion pictures I have made and the plays I have chosen to direct represent those convictions.

I have placed a copy of this affidavit with Mr. Spyros P. Skouras, president of 20th Century Fox.

Elia Kazan
Sworn to before me this 10th day of April, 1952

Mr. Tavenner: Mr. Kazan, the staff or members of the Committee may desire to recall you at some future time for the purpose of asking you to make further explanations of some of the matters contained in your sworn statement.

Mr. Kazan: I will be glad to do anything to help—anything you consider necessary or valuable.

Mr. Walter: Mr. Kazan, we appreciate your cooperation with our Committee. It is only through the assistance of people such as you that we have been able to make the progress that has been made in bringing the attention of the American people to the machinations of this Communist conspiracy for world domination.

* * *

In 1956, days before the marriage of Arthur Miller and Marilyn Monroe, the House Un-American Activities Committee subpoenaed Miller, who refused to provide the names of writers he reportedly met at one of two Communist writers' meetings he attended long years before. Chairman Walters of the HUAC sent word to Miller's lawyer that he would be inclined to cancel Miller's hearing if Monroe agreed to take a photo with him. Miller refused Walters's request. Instead, he testified before the committee, was considered noncompliant, and got cited for contempt. The Supreme Court later reversed that citation. Miller later wrote about the Red Scare in his 2000 essay "Are You Now or Have You Ever Been?":

> The heart of the darkness was the belief that a massive, profoundly organized conspiracy was in place and carried forward mainly by a concealed phalanx of intellectuals, including labor activists, teachers, professionals, sworn to undermine the American government. . . . The unwelcome truth denied by the right was that the Hollywood writers accused of subversion were not a menace to the country, or even bearers of meaningful change. They wrote not propaganda but entertainment, some of it of a mildly liberal cast, but most of it mindless, or when it was political, as with Preston Sturges or Frank Capra, entirely and exuberantly un-Marxist.
>
> As for the left, its unacknowledged truth was more important for me. If nobody was being shot in our ideological war but merely vivisected by a headline, it struck me as odd, if understandable, that the accused were unable to cry out passionately their faith in the ideals of socialism. There were attacks on the HUAC's right to demand that a citizen reveal his political beliefs; but on the idealistic canon of their own convictions, the defendants were mute.

A gulf opened between Miller and Kazan that took years to bridge. As Kazan went on to say about *The Hook*, "The thing just broke apart." One of several things that broke it apart was the statement Kazan published in *The New York Times* on April 12, 1952. Titled "A Statement by Elia Kazan," it reads:

> In the past weeks intolerable rumors about my political position have been circulating in New York and Hollywood. I want to make my stand clear:
>
> I believe that Communist activities confront the people of this country with an unprecedented and exceptionally tough problem. That is, how to protect ourselves from a dangerous and alien conspiracy and still keep the free, open, healthy ways of life that gives [*sic*] us self-respect.
>
> I believe that the American people can solve this problem wisely only if they have the facts about Communism. All the facts.
>
> Now I believe that any American who is in possession of such facts has the obligation to make them known, either to the public or to the appropriate Government agency.
>
> Whatever hysteria exists—and there is some, particularly in Hollywood—is inflamed by mystery, suspicion and secrecy. Hard and exact facts will cool it.
>
> The facts I have are sixteen years out of date, but they supply a small piece of background to the graver picture of communism today.
>
> I have placed these facts before the House Committee on Un-American Activities without reserve and I now place them before the public and before my co-workers in motion pictures and in the theatre.
>
> Seventeen and a half years ago I was a twenty-four-year old stage manager and bit actor, making $40 a week, when I worked.
>
> At that time nearly all of us felt menaced by two things: The depression and the ever growing power of Hitler. The streets were full of unemployed and shaken men. I was taken in by the

Hard Times version of what might be called the Communists' advertising or recruiting technique. They claimed to have a cure for depressions and a cure for Naziism and Fascism.

I joined the Communist Party late in the summer of 1934. I got out a year and a half later.

I have no spy stories to tell, because I saw no spies. Nor did I understand, at that time, any opposition between American and Russian national interest. It was not even clear to me in 1936, that the American Communist Party was abjectly taking its orders from the Kremlin.

What I learned was the minimum that anyone must learn who puts his head into the noose of party "discipline." The Communists automatically violated the daily practices of democracy to which I was accustomed. They attempted to control thought and to suppress personal opinion. They tried to dictate personal conduct. They habitually distorted and disregarded and violated the truth. All this was crudely opposite of their claims of "democracy" and "the scientific approach."

To be a member of the Communist Party is to have a taste of the police state. It is a diluted taste but it is bitter and unforgettable. It is diluted because you can walk out.

I got out in the spring of 1936.

The question will be asked why I did not tell this story sooner. I was held back, primarily, by concern for the reputations and employment of people who may, like myself, have left the party many years ago.

I was held back by a piece of specious reasoning which has silenced many liberals. It goes like this: "You may hate the Communists, but you must not attack or expose them, because if you do you are attacking the right to hold unpopular opinions and you are joining the people who attack civil liberties."

I have thought soberly about this. It is, simply, a lie.

Secrecy serves the Communists. At the other pole, it serves those who are interested in silencing liberal voices. The employment of a lot of good liberals is threatened because they have allowed themselves to become associated with or silenced by the Communists.

Liberals must speak out.

I think it is useful that certain of us had this kind of experience with the Communists, for if we had not we should not know them so well. Today, when all the world fears war and they scream peace, we know how much their professions are worth. We know tomorrow they will have a new slogan.

Firsthand experience of dictatorship and thought control left me with an abiding hatred of these. It left me with an abiding hatred of Communist philosophy and methods and the conviction that these must be resisted always.

It also left me with the passionate conviction that we must never let the Communists get away with the pretense that they stand for the very things which they kill in their own countries.

I am talking about free speech, a free press, the rights of property, the rights of labor, racial equality and, above all, individual rights. I value these things. I take them seriously. I value peace, too, when it is not bought at the price of fundamental decencies.

I believe these things must be fought for wherever they are not fully honored and protected whenever they are threatened.

The motion pictures I have made and the plays I have chosen to direct represent my convictions.

I expect to continue to make the same kinds of pictures and to direct the same kinds of plays.

## Budd Schulberg

In 1953, even with the rejections piled up for *The Hook* and with Kazan's naming names having made him a pariah in certain Hollywood circles, his career stock remained high. Studio bosses like Zanuck were regularly offering him $250,000 to direct films he turned down. But he knew that he needed an important and meaningful piece of material to get him back on track. His recent Broadway forays *Flight Into Egypt* and *Camino Real* had flopped. Critics and movie audiences had been reserved in appreciating his most recent films *Panic in the Streets*, *Viva Zapata!*, and *Man on a Tightrope*. Kazan hungered for personal and artistic redemption. After Arthur Miller, Kazan, on the suggestion of his wife, Molly, turned where smart directors always turn—to writers. As it had with Robert Siodmak before him, Kazan's road to redemption led to Budd Schulberg and Bucks County. Not only was Schulberg an estimable novelist and well connected in the movie industry, but he also, like Kazan, had informed on former Communist Party colleagues by corroborating the names of people already branded as Communists. Once a member of the Communist Party, Schulberg had left it after his 1944 novel *What Makes Sammy Run?* received heavy criticism from Hollywood Party members, including John Howard Lawson. Like Kazan, he remained unwavering in maintaining that he had done the right thing. Schulberg said of his 1951 testimony, "When I was asked by the HUAC, I felt that I couldn't just take the Fifth and not say anything. . . . You don't know what it was like being a member of the Communist Party. Each time you left the city, you had to inform them. They weren't a bunch of romantic people, but overcontrolling." Schulberg claimed that the Party pressured him to write certain works and not others, including in the latter category, his savage exposé of an ambitious young louse in Hollywood, *What Makes Sammy Run?*

Kazan was the right person to pay a visit to Schulberg at the right time. The writer had just completed his novel *The Disenchanted* and had no immediate idea for another. More importantly, this was Kazan, known for *Gentleman's Agreement*, *A Streetcar Named Desire*, and *Death of a Salesman*—not the kind of director who, as Schulberg put it, "never seemed to respect [the screenwriter] as the true source of the production." Not the kind of moviemaker, in other words, who had made the wised-up, hardboiled Schulberg flee Hollywood the way Dorothy Parker and Aldous Huxley, among others, had. Kazan proposed to Schulberg that they make a "non-Hollywood"–style film, birthed, written, and shot entirely on the East Coast. Kazan, he said, "came to me and said, 'If you write a screenplay, I'll treat you exactly like Arthur Miller and Tennessee Williams.' That won me." Kazan was preaching to the choir. As late as August 15, 2020, Schulberg told Gerald Peary in the online arts magazine *The Arts Fuse*, "It's bugged me since I was sixteen years old. It's an anti-writer culture and that goes all the way to the *New York Times*. Look in Arts & Leisure what is reviewed. [It] will say directed by, photographed by [but] there's no writer in that box."

Schulberg immediately offered that he'd been working for a long time on a waterfront story. There is reason to believe that Kazan shared the general ideas and themes that Miller and he had discussed for their own waterfront project. In any event, Schulberg gave Kazan his copies of Malcolm Johnson's "Crime on the Waterfront" stories along with the screenplay. For his part, Arthur Miller believed that Schulberg not only knew of his script but also that he may have read it even before Kazan approached him. Schulberg always denied this, calling it "coincidence" and "absolutely two separate, if overlapping, projects," and resented the implication that he created the script in imitation of Miller's writing style.

But initially, Kazan sent Schulberg down the road of investigating the dramatic potential of the real-life circumstances surrounding the 1948 murder of an elderly Trenton, New Jersey, secondhand furniture seller and the brutal assault on the victim's wife. Public pressure to find the perpetrator led to the warrantless arrest, four days of questioning without lawyers present, a trial, and a death sentence imposed by an all-white jury on six young black men who became known collectively as "The Trenton Six." Although Schulberg spent weeks in Trenton researching the incendiary events that sparked a civil rights outcry, in the end, he and Kazan decided that the subject was too rich and sprawling to confine to a two-hour movie.

Instead, they returned to the waterfront backdrop that had continued to compel them both. Although Harry Cohn's nephew had long ago reached out to Schulberg to gauge his interest in developing Malcolm Johnson's "Crime on the Waterfront" stories for films, that proposition had been crushed by Cohn's opposition. Schulberg was too wise to the ways of Hollywood moguls to let Cohn's opinion put him off the scent of a good story. This time, though, already thoroughly familiar with Johnson's work, Schulberg told Kazan that it was time for him to "go down to the docks" to experience firsthand the ramifications of New Jersey's and New York's 25,000 longshoremen desperate for work but being held hostage by mob denizens. Controlling Manhattan's Upper West Side was the Bowers family, while John M. "Cockeye" Dunn and Freddie McGurn ran the Lower West Side. Brooklyn was in the grip of the dreaded executioners, the Anastasia family. These mobsters, aided and abetted by the very people and agencies that should have been helping the exploited dockworkers, skimmed at least 10 percent of all harbor business while the wharf hiring bosses (also under the thumb of the Mafia) demanded kickbacks that left the workers scrambling for scraps.

Schulberg spent over a year in research. "Corruption on the waterfront became a cause for me," he said. "There was a priest on the West Side, Father Jack M. Corridan, who opposed the influence of organized crime. He said: 'Be our messenger.'" Infiltrating that closed world took some doing. Corridan, described by Schulberg as "a rangy, ruddy, fast-talking, chain-smoking, tough-minded, sometimes profane Kerryman," led Schulberg to fellow rebel, Little Arthur "Brownie" Browne, a longshoreman with a mashed nose, a fireplug build, and a Damon Runyon–style vocabulary. Over a series of long nights, Brownie acted as Schulberg's waterfront cicerone, guiding him to barrooms frequented by dockworkers, secretly pointing out key players, and hoping to allay their natural suspicion toward newcomers by introducing Schulberg as a fellow boxing fan from Stillman's Gym. With crowds this rough and potentially volatile, Browne kept his goal simple: get the men talking. Schulberg's directive: drink; listen; and, above all, ask no questions as they'd go prowling bucket-of-blood bars that ran as many as 10 to a block, mostly frequented by the second-generation Irish dockworkers. "The waterfront wasn't what you'd call mixed. It was almost 100 per cent second-generation Irish. No Italians, even. But I fitted in well. I have a knack for that. Maybe the stammer helped." The poison of choice was a boilermaker (beer with a shot of whiskey). One night, bouncing from bar to bar, Schulberg, on his fifth boilermaker, asked a serious-looking man in a gray suit what he did for a living. In nothing flat, Brownie yanked Schulberg out of his seat and sent them both running for four blocks, asking, "Jesus, Mary 'n Joseph, you wanna get us both killed?" Once they were a safe distance, he explained that the guy that had sent them running was only one of the most vicious gangsters on the waterfront, an Albert Anastasia wannabe killer who'd broken Brownie's nose and dropped him through a skylight and, another time, tossed him, unconscious, into the wintry river. A week earlier, the same man had killed a dock boss. It was hardly his first time.

Schulberg and Kazan decided early on Hoboken, New Jersey, as the right location for their narrative and for filming. The decision posed an immediate challenge, said Kazan in the 1970s. "The actors had to be in the same league as the scenery. They had to be as real as Hoboken." Authenticity became the guiding principle. One of Schulberg's earliest ideas for a central character was to pattern the character Terry Malloy after reporter Malcom Johnson. That Terry Malloy would have been a tough, cynical newspaper man, an investigative reporter who finds an ally in "the waterfront priest" based on Father

John Corridan. To that end, Schulberg brought along Kazan to first-hand observe Corridan, who met the oppressed dockworkers on their home turf—barrooms, alleys, and rallies at his parish church, St. Xavier's. Kazan marveled as Corridan railed not only against the mobsters but also against uber-reactionary arch hypocrite Cardinal Spellman for recommending the Catholic Church's highest honor for the likes of dock denizen Bill McCormack. After all, McCormack, whom Schulberg dubbed "Mister Big" of the waterfront, was a man who openly demanded a piece of everything that moved in and out of New York's docks and made a lapdog of Joe Ryan, the International Longshoreman of America president. After witnessing Father John's rafter-raising meeting at St. Xavier's, Kazan turned to Schulberg and asked, "Are you sure he's a priest? . . . Maybe's he's working there for the waterfront rebels in disguise." Schulberg joked to Kazan that he'd been seeing too many Hollywood movies, but they both, writer and director, knew that in Brownie, McCormack, and Father Corridan they had the basis for three compelling characters for the new scenario that had begun evolving in their work sessions.

Kazan became especially excited by Schulberg's gift for finding poetry in the jargon of the dockworkers he observed. He grew even more encouraged when the writer shared verbatim this section of a speech Father Corridan gave to longshoremen in the hold of a cargo ship in the union's trade school in New Jersey: "I suppose some people would smirk at the thought of Christ in the shape-up. It is about as absurd as the fact He carried a carpenter's tools in His hands and earned His bread by the sweat of His brow. As absurd as the fact that Christ redeemed all men irrespective of their race, color, or station in life. It can be absurd only to those of whom Christ has said, 'Having eyes, they do see not; and having ears, they hear not.' Because they don't want to see or hear. Christ also said, 'If you do it to the least of mine, then you do it to me.' So Christ is in the shape-up." In Schulberg's screenplay, the character would say:

Boys, this is my church. If you don't think Christ is here on the waterfront, you got another guess coming. And who do you think he lines up with? Every morning when the hiring boss blows his whistle, Jesus stands alongside you in the shape-up. He sees why some of you get picked and some of you get passed over. He sees the family men worrying about getting their rent and getting food in the house for the wife and kids. He sees them selling their souls to the mob for a day's pay. What does Christ think of the easy-money boys who do none of the work and take all the gravy? What does He think of these fellows wearing hundred-and-fifty-dollar suits and diamond rings—on your union dues and your kickback money? How does He feel about bloodsuckers picking up a longshoreman's work tab and grabbing twenty percent interest at the end of the week? How does He, who spoke up without fear against evil, feel about your silence? . . . But remember, fellows, Christ is always with you—Christ is in the shape-up. He's in the hatch. He's in the union hall.

Said Schulberg, who called Corridan "the greatest individual I have ever known," "the speech was written more by [him] than me. Eighty percent of it was his words."

For Schulberg, the research proved invaluable, and he'd spend the end of every night at the kitchen table in Brownie and his wife Anne's cold-water flat, where he lived while doing his research. There, he'd write down "dialogue" he had heard that day. Some of that dialogue, and a bit more, may have come by way of Anthony "Tony Mike" DeVincenzo, a young Italian immigrant and Hoboken local whom Schulberg met through Brownie. Not only was DeVincenzo a longshoreman and stevedore hiring boss but also, briefly, a professional boxer who happened to raise pigeons for a hobby. In 1950, after two decades working the docks, he refused to stifle his outrage over the corruption he saw all around him as exemplified by the practices of ILA organizer Edward J. Florio. In 1952, DeVincenzo became a key witness in the investigations held by the New York State Waterfront Crime Commission. Whistleblowing cost him his job. He later became a park superintendent and part owner of a restaurant and, according to some, wound up as a street-corner newspaper salesman. "I was proud to be a rat," DeVincenzo maintained and never backed down. Small wonder that Schulberg promptly introduced him to Kazan, both of whom dined several times at DeVincenzo's Hoboken home while imbibing the former dockworker's stories. Said Kazan, "He went through the exact same experiences and he would tell me what he went through and what he felt and about the scorn thrown at him. I'd had a good deal of scorn thrown at me in those years. I was hefty. I could take it. He was, too. He was tough and he was ready to fight all the time. That helped a lot, seeing this man who went through the whole damn thing that our story was going to be about. He was in a fury about it. . . . I did see Tony Mike's story as my own." Overnight, his and Schulberg's work on the script's central character became even more intensely personal.

In later years, though, Schulberg would downplay DeVincenzo's influence on the character of Terry Malloy and on the movie in general, instead citing Malcolm Johnson's articles as his primary source of inspiration. However, in an interview Schulberg gave in 2000, when asked directly about DeVincenzo, he acknowledged "there were some similarities and Tony Mike's life did overlap with the story and character I had written." Not altogether unsurprisingly, after the release of *On the Waterfront*, DeVincenzo would sue Sam Spiegel and the releasing studio for invasion of privacy. Although the moviemakers contended that the film was purely a work of fiction, Marlon Brando testified that he had been specifically instructed by Kazan that if he accepted the role of Terry Malloy, he should meet with DeVincenzo. Speaking of DeVincenzo's lawsuit, Schulberg said in 2000, "No one wanted to be contentious."

In the end, DeVincenzo won a judgment of $22,000, a lot less than the $1 million for which he had asked.

Schulberg devoted over one year to his research while working out with Kazan the characters, story, themes, imagery, and more. They would meet for work sessions either at Kazan's 212 East 72nd Street townhouse or at Schulberg's Bucks County farm. "It was more than research. I became involved with the movement on the waterfront," Schulberg said. As part of his commitment to the cause and the project, Schulberg wrote articles advocating for the rebel longshoreman movement for *The New York Times* and the *Saturday Evening Post*. Citing Schulberg's "extraordinary commitment" to the work and to the cause, Kazan said, "We worked on the script together. It was a great experience. I used to hang out in Hoboken but not like Budd did. Budd was there all the time. Budd lived there. It was a great, great writing experience for me to watch him put that film together. He never stopped working." Schulberg not only dove deeply into his source material, but he also shared strong ideas about casting. For example, he approached friend and colleague John Garfield, the impassioned and politically progressive stage and film star, about playing the lead role of Terry. "He would have been good, maybe great," observed Schulberg of the actor, arguably best known to 1940s moviegoers for his roles in *The Postman Always Rings Twice*, *Humoresque*, and *Body and Soul*, for which he was nominated for a Best Actor Academy Award.

Kazan, who knew Garfield from the Group Theater days, appreciated the actor's worth as an artist and a box-office booster. Kazan had also directed him in *Gentleman's Agreement*, his 1947 Best Picture Oscar winner. In the same year and for similar reasons, Broadway producer Irene Mayer Selznick had all but set Garfield to play Stanley Kowalski in *A Streetcar Named Desire*. Garfield, more a movie star than a stage actor at that point, refused to commit beyond a four-month run. He also wanted first refusal of playing Kowalski in the event of a movie version. Kazan told Selznick that he was fine with Garfield, but he kept angling for Brando, believing the lesser-known, decade-younger actor would give New York audiences the thrill of discovering a theatrical and sexual lightning rod. "If I can avoid casting a star, that's what I'll do," Kazan said. But there was also this: Garfield's impassioned left-leaning politics had begun to attract scrutiny from the House Un-American Activities Committee, and the stress of his being hounded by them contributed to his death at age 39 in 1952. Said Schulberg, "[His] career and life were being destroyed by his pathetically 'Un-American Activities' and he died of a heart attack before our project was underway." During Garfield's funeral service at Riverside Memorial Chapel, some 10,000 people lined Amsterdam and 76th Streets, prompting newspapers to call it the largest public outpouring for an actor since the death of Rudolph Valentino in 1926.

# Two

# Darryl Zanuck vs. the Sweaty Longshoremen

In early 1952, Schulberg excitedly presented his screenplay draft to Kazan, who, according to Schulberg, read and immediately pronounced it "one of the three best I ever had. And the other two were *Death of a Salesman* and *Streetcar Named Desire*." Kazan, who owed a film to Darryl F. Zanuck at Fox, enthused to Schulberg that they had to approach the excitable mogul even though he had earlier turned down the project. Besides, Kazan believed that the script was now immeasurably improved. He crowed, "This is just the thing for Zanuck. This is right down Zanuck's line. He loves violent stories about big cities." Kazan's optimism and myopia are easily traced. In 1945, the feared and respected Zanuck had brought the former actor turned theatrical giant to the studio to handle *A Tree Grows in Brooklyn*. Kazan warned him that he could not make a movie "unless I have some empathy with the basic theme." Zanuck told Kazan that no matter what he thought of Betty Smith's hugely popular sentimental novel about the aspirations and challenges faced by a poor Irish family living in the Williamsburg neighborhood in 1912, Zanuck had won the film rights in a heated bidding war and was throwing the full weight of the studio behind the fledgling Kazan to direct it. The film went on to big box-office success and earned multiple Oscar wins. Kazan became one of Zanuck's heroes, and as a reward, Zanuck handed him the director's reins on the "issue film" *Gentleman's Agreement*, from Laura Z. Hobson's novel about American antisemitism. The movie brought eight Academy Award nominations and Kazan his first Best Director Oscar. *Pinky*, the all-too-rare early Hollywood film to dramatize racial prejudice and bigotry, further burnished Kazan's brand.

In the late fall of 1952, Kazan urged Schulberg to send Zanuck his 37-page outline with dialogue titled *The Bottom of the River*, a more detailed version of the original April 1951 version titled *Crime on the Waterfront* and, later, *Waterfront*. In response, Kazan recalled Zanuck saying, "I'll make some suggestions and he did." Long distance, Schulberg worked on the screenplay with Zanuck, who, according to Kazan, was nothing but encouraging and supportive. Satisfied and optimistic, Kazan fired off to Zanuck what Schulberg called a "Here we come!" letter. As the pair boarded the Super Chief for the trip west, Kazan tried to buoy Schulberg's battered optimism about the whole enterprise. "We had chosen a tough subject," Schulberg said. "We had taken real characters and put them through a struggle that was still being waged. Was it too somber, too real for the Hollywood Dream Machine?" Kazan countered that Zanuck, unlike other studio moguls, had stepped up to the challenges of making movies out of "tough subjects," including *The Grapes of Wrath*, *How Green Was My Valley*, and *Pinky*. Besides, Kazan told Schulberg, "I don't think you realize how great this is . . . *Salesman* . . . *Streetcar* . . . *Waterfront*."

But when the Super Chief pulled into the station in downtown Los Angeles, no studio limousine awaited them. When they checked into their Beverly Hills Hotel suite, there were no welcoming note, basket of flowers, bottles of champagne, or obligatory fruit basket. Wrote Schulberg years later, "I had been raised in Hollywood. I knew the unspoken language. No limo and no roses, no loving welcome, and no invitation to come down to Palm Springs for the big Sunday croquet match spelled big trouble." In fact, Schulberg and Kazan whiled away the weekend playing tennis and commandeering the best table at the Polo Lounge without a word from Zanuck. An early Monday morning phone call to Zanuck's office advised them that the boss was still busy playing croquet; they would be called to set up an official appointment. "Darryl hates it or he would have called us from Palm Springs to say hello," Schulberg said. "Let's not jump to conclusions," Kazan said, but this time, with more bravado than assurance.

That afternoon the men sat parked in the anteroom of Zanuck's office. As Kazan well knew, beyond the secretaries and the big wood doors lay Zanuck's private lair. Spacious, wood paneled, floors and walls decorated with the hypermasculine mogul's safari bagatelle and taxidermy and polo trophies, this office was notorious. The wall behind Zanuck's desk housed locked wooden compartments, sliding doors of which revealed shelves of expensive Parisian perfume, jewels, gloves, silk scarves, and stockings. These were gifts for Zanuck's other favorite species of prey, female stars and starlets. Unabashedly displayed on his desk sat a solid gold paperweight replica cast of his phallus. It was common studio knowledge that at specific times of the day, the legendarily priapic studio boss was strictly off limits to anyone but one of his stable of female contract players. "In conference," he would lock his office doors from inside, forbid any interruption, and demand sexual services from the young woman who may leave with a plum role in a new movie, a gift, both, or nothing but a promise and a demand for another session.

Accordingly, Schulberg and Kazan, who had already been awaiting their audience with Zanuck for a half hour or so, knew what to expect when into the waiting room strode Bajla Węgier, a 24-year-old Polish stage performer and actress whom Zanuck and his wife, Virginia, had picked up on the Riviera, paid-off her considerable gambling debts, and impulsively invited to live with them in America. The smitten Zanucks renamed her Bella Darvi (her last name a combination of the names "Darryl" and "Virginia"), and in 1953,

Zanuck signed her to a long-term 20th Century Fox contract. Publicly, Zanuck announced his plans to pair Darvi and Richard Widmark in an adventure film *Hell and High Water* for director Samuel Fuller, then step things up, at least budget-wise, by casting her (not Marilyn Monroe, who wanted the role) opposite Marlon Brando in the historical epic *The Egyptian*, Zanuck's sole personally supervised prestige production of the year. Darvi, Zanuck's latest mistress and personal "discovery," became the object of his obsession to turn her into a major star. Kazan and Schulberg exchanged looks while Darvi got buzzed into bounty hunter Zanuck's pleasure dome. They knew they'd be waiting awhile longer. What they didn't know was that Zanuck, who had lost a bundle on Kazan and Brando's *Viva Zapata!*, was fuming over the very public rumors that Brando was dreading the prospect of having to fulfill his contractual commitment to star in *The Egyptian*. He thought the script and role absurd, nor did he welcome the prospect of working with authoritarian tough guy director Michael Curtiz or the inexperienced, modestly talented Bella Darvi.

After Darvi had let herself out of the conveniently located discreet rear door of Zanuck's lair, Kazan and Schulberg got ushered in. Zanuck launched into a paean to Hollywood technical innovations from the silent era and sound through Technicolor and the super wide screen processes that were expected to bring back to theaters audiences who had defected to television. (He apparently omitted Bela Darvi among those innovations.) He rhapsodized about an upcoming comic strip–based Robert Wagner–Janet Leigh extravaganza: "Can you imagine how *Prince Valiant* is going to be in Cinemascope? All those beautiful broads in silky gowns practically on top of you! I tell you; this is an exciting business!" Kazan repeatedly tried to shift the discussion to his and Schulberg's small-scale, gritty black-and-white movie. Finally, Zanuck answered that he had read Schulberg's revisions. His verdict? "I'm sorry, but I didn't like a single thing about it." Kazan's stage-trained voice boomed as he launched his impassioned defense of the script, comparing the endurance of the oppressed longshoremen to the endurance of the oppressed Oakies in Zanuck's beloved and respected *The Grapes of Wrath*; Zanuck shot back, "But the Oakies came across like American pioneers! This is exactly what audiences don't want to see now. Who's going to give a shit about a lot of sweaty longshoremen?" Kazan even tried pitching their hero Terry as a young FBI agent; Zanuck saw right through it. In the end, Zanuck said, "If you come to me with this story in this present state and you say, 'I have got Marlon Brando for this picture,' then it is a simple decision to make." But they most certainly did not have Brando, and Zanuck knew it.

Schulberg reflected, "Zanuck really balled him out. He said, 'Gadg, I think you're a great talent but there's something wrong with you. Why do you want to do these crazy movies? First, you bring me *Viva Zapata!* and now you bring me this? Really, what is wrong with you?' I sat there listening to this and it was really demeaning, you know? It stabbed me in the heart. Look, you can't name a studio that didn't turn us down—Paramount, Warner Bros., 20th Century Fox, Columbia, MGM. They not only turned it down, but they also insulted it. 'Why do you want to do this thing?' I mean, they'd ball out Kazan as they did it."

A meeting that Kazan thought would focus on such details as shooting schedules, casting, and other production minutiae ended instead with yelling, cross accusations, recriminations, and warnings about betrayals of trust and broken contracts. Enraged, Schulberg and Kazan left the meeting and made straight for the office Zanuck had given them for the *Waterfront* they apparently weren't delivering. There, Kazan and Schulberg let loose their frustrations by upending a desk and hurling chairs and telephones before decamping with a typewriter and armfuls of office supplies. On the taxi ride back to the Beverly Hills Hotel, Kazan reminded Schulberg that his directorial talents remained a viable Hollywood commodity and surely Jack Warner would be the right executive for *Waterfront*. "Don't tell me, tell him," Schulberg fired back, increasingly weary of Kazan's pep talks.

Back in their hotel room, Schulberg listened as Kazan pitched Jack Warner by phone, hitting all the high notes. *Powerful story. The kind of movie Warner does better than anyone else. Waterfront is like something from the glory days of the studio's hard-hitting Public Enemy and I Am a Fugitive From a Chain Gang.* Then came the "buts" and the defensive maneuvers as Kazan struggled to gain ground. *It's about more than the labor struggle. No, it isn't grim. There is a love story!* Long before the click of the phone, Schulberg gave up on Warner Bros., and on the next day both MGM and Paramount. Schulberg recalls he and Kazan "pacing up and down in their bathrobes, all day, all night," ashamed to accept friends' invitations to dine at this or that famed Hollywood watering hole. Wrote Schulberg, "Anybody who's ever worked in Hollywood knows how tough it is to go out on the town a loser. In my hometown, losing and leprosy are interchangeable." They were dead men walking, especially when the *Hollywood Reporter's* gossip columnist printed an especially bilious item about how every studio in town was steering clear of the project because it was rife with radicalism and Communism.

# THREE

# The Spiegel Catalog

They continued working on the screenplay, rewriting, pruning, and creating new scenes and plot complications. Their hotel suite told the story. Discarded script pages littered the carpets. Room service trays lined the tabletops. Around the time Kazan and Schulberg began kicking around the idea of mounting *Waterfront* for the stage, Zanuck stopped paying their expenses. Kazan declared, "God dammit I'm going to stick with this thing if I have to get a 16-millimeter newsreel camera and shoot it myself down at the docks." Enter international producer Sam Spiegel, formerly known as S. P. Eagle, who knew about career ups and downs, having followed the brilliant success of *The African Queen* with *Melba*, an operatic biographical stinker so bad that theater owners refused to book it. Spiegel lived as large when saddled with a flop as he did during greener times, and he knew how to deal with Kazan and Schulberg.

Weary of the gentlemen turning down his invitations to cross the corridor and join one of his lush, sybaritic parties of Dom Perignon, beautiful women, and major stars and directors, he knocked on their door. Sizing up the depth of their depression evident in their slovenly bathrobes, unkempt appearance, and stubble, he popped open their door and asked, "Are you guys in trouble?" Were they *ever*. Gore Vidal observed that Spiegel had a "truffle nose" for finding major talent on the skids, largely because he knew he could probably get them to work at fire sale rates.

Of the many things that Hollywood has had to say about the *larger* than larger-than-life independent film producer Sam Spiegel, few have been flattering. First, though, here is something indisputably true—and pleasant—about him. "The last authentic movie tycoon" is how film historian and documentarian Kevin Brownlow aptly described Spiegel, a titan who never owned or ran a film studio and yet produced such financially successful creative milestones of the 1950s and 1960s as *The African Queen*, *The Bridge on the River Kwai*, and *Lawrence of Arabia*.

But David Lean, who directed the latter two classics to a total of 14 Academy Award wins and today's equivalent of $1.2 billion in profits, termed Spiegel "a dictator with no respect for human dignity and individuality." Director John Huston cursed his decision to join forces with Spiegel on a company called Horizon Pictures when, in 1951, their audience favorite joint effort *The African Queen* created such a box-office windfall that Spiegel helped himself to Huston's deferred salary of 50 percent of the film's profits as well as the 25 percent owed the film's stars Humphrey Bogart and the 10 percent due to Katharine Hepburn. Meanwhile, Spiegel could not resist boasting to friends that his *The African Queen* earnings financed his famously lavish New Year's Eve parties catered by the world's greatest restaurants, let alone his long stays at the finest hotels, endless supplies of Cuban cigars, insatiable appetite for women, and growing collection of fine art. Meanwhile, and with total impunity, Spiegel lowballed actors out of their usual salaries by promising to leave them in his will this or that masterwork from his collection of pieces by Degas, Gaugin, Kokoschka, Monet, Matisse, Picasso, Bonnard, Cezanne, and Toulouse-Lautrec. He never followed through. When Katharine Hepburn completed a film with him, she spat in his eye. Thanks to Spiegel's finagling, the first royalty check that composer Maurice Jarre received for his monumental and widely acclaimed *Lawrence of Arabia* score—a whopping $2.53—arrived a decade after the movie debuted. So outlandishly persuasive was this "congenital crook with a crook's mentality," as German screenwriter-director Gottfried Reinhardt dubbed Spiegel, that he even convinced Gore Vidal to write a screenplay for a second film because, quipped Vidal, "I couldn't believe it the first time." Director Billy Wilder likened the silver-tongued con man to a modern Robin Hood who "steals from the rich and steals from the poor."

He'd gotten an early start. Born November 11, 1901, in Jarosław, Poland, Spiegel was the son of a successful tobacco merchant and a soldier in the Austro-Hungarian army. Enterprising, bright, and confident, he studied at Vienna University and became a Zionist youth organization leader. In 1927, he married and soon abandoned his well-born young wife and their infant daughter in Europe, also leaving behind a mountain of debts. For over a decade after, he flitted from country to country using phony passports and occasionally producing forgettable films in Germany, Austria, Britain, and France. Though he lacked any demonstrable or consistent means of income, he managed to live like a raja. Putting to use his fluency in nine languages, he did movie translation work in America and England but got jailed in both countries for fraud and passing bad checks. By the time of the Nazi rise to power and the outbreak of World War II, he escaped Europe ("So what if I lied? I would have been a bar of soap," he told a friend) and hid out in Mexico, managing to stay only a few steps ahead of the law. He finagled his way back into the United States in 1939, illegally, of course—some think he did it by swimming the Rio Grande River— and retained the pseudonym S. P. Eagle. The year 1942 brought the first of S. P. Eagle's coproduced American feature films, *Tales of Manhattan*, for 20th Century Fox. Before the end of the decade, it was followed by the John Huston–directed Cuban adventure misfire *We Were Strangers*; *The Stranger*, an underestimated Orson Welles thriller about the hunt for a fugitive Nazi in a small town; and the fascinating and gamey low-budget thriller *The Prowler*, directed by Joseph Losey.

Secretly, the producer was also circling the drain. Yes, he had made certain that he, not Bogart, Hepburn, or John Huston, reaped all the profits from *The African Queen*. But he brought his personal finances and professional profile crashing down by leaning into a dull, highly fictionalized cinematic biography *Melba*, featuring young Metropolitan Opera star Patrice Munsel as the renowned Victorian-era and early 20th-century Australian-born lyric coloratura soprano opera diva. Plagued from the start, the moribund movie's embarrassing failure sped up Spiegel's eviction from his Grosvenor Square apartment for long-unpaid rent. Meanwhile, his years of philandering and grifting had made him *persona non grata* at his 6,000-square-foot Beverly Hills home at 702 N. Crescent Drive, where he faced arrest there at any moment. Also, he had served divorce papers on his wife, actress Lynne Baggett, whom he had met during her screen test for his 1945 movie *The Stranger* and to whom he had been married since 1948. The divorce papers accused Lynne, 20 years younger than Spiegel, of infidelity, which was, in fact, true. While Spiegel was in London during the making of *The African Queen* and reportedly bedding scores of women, Lynne and novelist-screenwriter Irwin Shaw had a brief affair, which Lynne followed by another affair, this time with *The African Queen* helmer John Huston. Isn't it rich? Such an indignity befalling "The Velvet Octopus," nicknamed for his insatiable appetite for women, including the expectation that actresses, especially young ones, grant him sexual favors if they expected to advance their careers. Spiegel's divorce deposition accused Lynne of having shattered every crystal glass and mirror in their Beverly Hills manse and slashed with scissors his bespoke suits, silk underwear, and several of his paintings, including six Picassos. "He always deflected," said actress Evelyn Keyes, an ex-Mrs. John Huston who starred in *The Prowler*, "If Sam stabbed you in the back, he would smile and try to convince you that he did it for your own good."

When the hounds nip at one's heels, a mere mortal might be tempted to sequester. Spiegel's idea of laying low was to install himself in a premier suite at the Beverly Hills Hotel and let nothing rain on his parade, not even *Melba*. And damn United Artists, its distributor, and damn Lynne. In the room across the hall from Spiegel were Kazan and Schulberg licking their wounds and wondering if there was any pulse left in their project, now retitled *The Golden Warrior*. Spiegel had repeatedly invited the men to his endless slate of lavish parties populated by show business movers and shakers, famous faces, and beautiful women (famous or not). If Kazan had been in better spirits, he might have accepted. He, like so many others, found Spiegel to be a fascinating buccaneer, roué, enigma, and opportunist. In fact, Kazan had met Spiegel when the producer had been hosting lavish parties in honor of John Huston and Olivia de Havilland (Huston's lover at the time) as a ploy to get to Huston to direct *The African Queen*. Kazan made the guest list due to his Oscar and box-office success, and Spiegel gave him carte blanche to use the tennis court at his Beverly Hills home, where the refrigerator was stocked with Moët & Chandon splits. "Everything Sam did was tactical," Kazan observed, adding, "but I had the impression that Sam didn't have a cent to his name."

Schulberg answered when Spiegel knocked on the door, meticulously groomed, sporting a midnight blue Savile Row suit, and smelling of, the writer recalled, "expensively crushed French lilacs." The producer's shark-eyed gaze scanned the wreckage of the Kazan-Schulberg suite: two unshaven, demoralized-looking men in rumpled bathrobes, leftover room service trays, and carpets strewn with script pages. Said Schulberg, "We were in bathrobes because we were so demoralized by our rejection. We could barely move or speak. We didn't know what to do. But Sam Spiegel was there, I knew him slightly, and he kept sending messages inviting Gadg and me to the party that never ended. No sooner than he asked, "Are you boys in trouble?" he invited Schulberg to pitch him *The Golden Warrior* story the following morning. Kazan and Schulberg had scheduled 8:00 a.m. checkouts and early morning flights back home for the following day. Spiegel advised Schulberg to arrive at 7:00 and said that he would leave his door unlocked so he wouldn't have to get out of bed. Then he vanished, leaving Kazan and Schulberg to wonder if all this was for real. Everyone in show business had heard hair-raising Spiegel stories. But Kazan and Schulberg were fresh out of options. Kazan called his agent at the William Morris office and received the obligatory warning, "Watch out for Sam! He has moves that you've never seen before."

At 7:00 on the dot the next morning, Schulberg, script tucked under his arm, found Spiegel—all five feet nine, two hundred pounds of him—reclined motionless on the double bed with eyes shut and the covers up to his chin. "It was like he was lying in state," Schulberg recalled. Pressed for time and greeted only by snores and grunts, Schulberg launched into *The Golden Warrior*, pacing the floor and occasionally saying "Sam? . . . Sam?," only to get a noncommittal "Hmmm." Whether or not Spiegel listened fully to the writer's impassioned performance of the script, when Schulberg was finished, Spiegel lifted his head slightly and announced on the spot, "I'll do it. We'll make the picture." Spiegel delivered the news to Kazan, who responded, "Sam's down on his uppers and doesn't have a red cent to his name. But watch that slippery fuck get this movie made!"

True to his word, that same morning, Spiegel messengered *The Golden Warrior* to Harry Cohn at Columbia. That's right, Harry Cohn, the same studio chief and crude vulgarian who had turned down the project earlier. And the same Cohn, who in 1956, on first hearing that his East Coast Columbia colleagues had agreed to finance Spiegel and David Lean's *The Bridge on the River Kwai*, bellowed, "How can you idiots in the New York office give a crook like Sam Spiegel $2 million and let him go off and shoot in some place like Ceylon?"

Cohn didn't give an immediate response, but no matter. By late morning, Spiegel and Schulberg were sharing a flight east, and by the time of their arrival in New York, Spiegel had already brokered a tentative deal with Arthur B. Krim, Robert Benjamin, and Matty Fox of United Artists, most recently successful with producer-director Stanley Kramer's *High Noon* and Spiegel and John Huston's partnership on *The African Queen* and *Moulin Rouge*. In the United Artists offices on Fifth Avenue, Spiegel listened when Krim insisted that to close the United Artists deal, he must first repay a $50,000 debt on the ill-fated *Melba* as well as pay off any outstanding loans and debts on *The Golden Warrior*. The meeting concluded with Krim believing the deal would be signed in a matter of days. Instead, Spiegel immediately headed to the Columbia Pictures executive offices in the same building. Within days, Columbia's attorneys finalized a deal to wrangle *On the Waterfront* from United Artists and instead swap the rights to the high-flying circus movie *Trapeze* starring Burt Lancaster and Tony Curtis. What's more, by undercutting United Artists and working out a deal with Columbia's completely independent New York office, Spiegel froze Harry Cohn out of *The Golden Warrior* since, like it or not, his domain was strictly the Hollywood office. Further distancing Cohn from the project, Spiegel—who disdained Cohn, who, in turn, resented him—moved his Horizon Pictures office from Hollywood to 424 Madison Avenue. As Kazan said then and would go on to acknowledge: "The fact is that the movie wouldn't have gotten made without Sam." And that was not just because of the project itself but also because Kazan and Schulberg had been among HUAC's friendliest of friendly witnesses, unlike other creators with whom Kazan had already worked, including Arthur Laurents and Dalton Trumbo. In the coming weeks and months, they would wonder time and again if the devil's bargain they struck was worth the price. The problems began with casting, which ended the project's short-lived honeymoon with United Artists.

# FOUR

# Casting "A Wiry, Jaunty Waterfront Hanger-On Whistling a Familiar Irish Song"

## *Searching for Terry Malloy*

In one draft of his screenplay, Budd Schulberg introduces the film's central figure, Terry Malloy, as "a wiry, jaunty waterfront hanger-on whistling a familiar Irish song." Does the body or spirit of Marlon Brando spring to mind from that description? Not necessarily. Yet Brando's casting would go on to be considered a masterstroke. And his performance—tragic, poetic, charming, brutish, boyish, idiosyncratic, sensual, heartbreaking, and funny—would go on to be considered one of the glories of American cinema. As Martin Scorsese would say several decades after seeing the movie for the first time, "It had a direct line for the truth of the way people think, the way people behave, the way people live and how and where they live. Everything from the texture of the walls in the bar, the bartender's shirt, everything, is literally as if it was shot on Elizabeth Street, Mott Street or Mulberry Street. Whether they're Irish names, Italian names doesn't matter. The character of Terry Malloy [was] very close to people I knew, people I lived with." Alec Baldwin, who essayed another iconic Brando role alongside Jessica Lange in a 1992 Broadway revival of *A Streetcar Named Desire*, said, "You watch Brando in *Waterfront* knowing that he's not just hitting every conceivable note, he's an entire symphony." Al Pacino said, "He pinned me to my theater seat. I was so devastated by him, I literally couldn't move after the movie was over." Elia Kazan said in his 1976 biography, "If there's a better performance by a man in the history of film in America, I don't know what it is."

Movie casting that clicks the way Brando's does in *On the Waterfront* seems predestined. But when the project was in its earliest stages of casting, Brando's participation looked anything but solid. Of course, in the early 1950s, Brando was a name to be reckoned with and a presence virtually everyone wanted to cast in a movie. The actor had been making noise in the theater world since his Broadway debut at age 23 in the long-running hit *I Remember Mama* in 1946. The restless actor didn't stay with the show for long, instead joining the casts of four successive shows the same year. One nationally syndicated columnist called him at the time, "A legend in the making . . . [a]nd his poet's face, football player's physique and volcanic personality have made him a perfect figure around which to build that legend." Brando stoked the legend, whether he intended to or not. Hollywood heard tales of how no less than the vaunted acting team of Alfred Lunt and Lynn Fontanne kept asking him to speak up during a theater audition until he pretty much told them where to stick their play and ambled off. About how, after auditioning for Noël Coward's *Present Laughter*, he hurled the script and stormed out asking whether the author was aware that there was such a thing in the world as people starving. In 1947, he made his reputation in *A Streetcar Named Desire* while his costar Jessica Tandy cited his chronic lateness, difficulty learning lines, and playing his role differently every performance according to his mercurial moods as the mark of "an impossible, psychopathic bastard." She couldn't grasp what she was witnessing. As Kazan put it, "Hers was a performance. Marlon was living on stage." Hollywood felt the heat and, by 1953, had attempted to capture him on celluloid in *The Men*, *A Streetcar Named Desire*, *Viva Zapata!*, *Julius Caesar*, and *The Wild One*. The more film contracts the big shots waved in front of him, the more roles he turned down—*High Noon*, *Senso*, and *Sudden Fear* among them. That only made them want him more. Brando felt trapped by having been persuaded by Darryl F. Zanuck to sign a multiple film deal with 20th Century Fox.

Said actor and Kazan confidante Karl Malden, who had appeared in several Kazan-directed movies and plays, including *A Streetcar Named Desire*, "Pretty early on, Kazan told me a great deal about his waterfront project and how Sam Spiegel wanted Marlon Brando to play Terry Malloy. I was more than interested in being a part of it. Kazan also told me that Brando had said no when he got the script because he wouldn't bring himself to work with a squealer, someone who had done what Kazan had done—naming names during the McCarthy era. Marlon simply refused on that principle. He had dug his heels in. And so, it became clear to us that if the picture was going to be made, it would be without Marlon." Spiegel asked Malden to intervene with Brando. Malden said, "There was a long period when Marlon wasn't going to do it. . . . Marlon and I knew each other well from doing *A Streetcar Named Desire*. . . . I told him, 'Marlon, you're judging who is right and wrong . . . don't try and play God because it's going to hit you.'"

When Columbia's executives asked Sam Spiegel which actor he and Elia Kazan had in mind for the leading role, it wasn't an idle question. The budget hinged on their casting a bankable name. Sam Spiegel's first thought was Frank Sinatra, born and raised in Hoboken and, at the time, not as incongruous an idea as it might sound today. Spiegel, nobody's fool, understood that Hollywood loves few things more than a comeback saga. Sinatra had pulled off the biggest of his day. In the early 1950s, his movie career was on the rocks, his heartbreaker's croon had been eroded by vocal wear and tear, and his emotions made even more volatile than usual thanks to his turbulent marriage to tempestuous movie siren Ava Gardner. But by 1953, Sinatra was back in demand after his acclaimed *From Here to Eternity* performance that went on to win him an Oscar. The actor was hungry for another powerhouse film role and, perceiving Schulberg's script (now simply called *Waterfront*) as a tougher, latter-day *Going My Way*, he thought this was it. Kazan signed off on Sinatra's casting. "Sam did call me on the phone one day and say that I might have a chat with Sinatra," recalled Kazan. "I knew—and believe now—that I could make the picture with Frank and that he'd be fine in the role." Kazan and the notoriously prickly Sinatra had their conversation and agreed on costuming for his character. Said the director, "He knew the territory and, of course, having grown up in Hoboken, he spoke perfect Hobokenese." The singer's agents informed Spiegel and Kazan that their client's preexisting concert and film commitments limited his availability to 27 days in November. Despite Kazan's warning that they might be being played, Spiegel and Sinatra struck what Schulberg called "a handshake deal."

Not long after hearing the news, Kazan told Spiegel that it might not be worth gambling on Sinatra's real or imagined schedule limitations. Spiegel advised him not to worry, then one day asked how he'd like having Marlon Brando in the movie instead. Kazan called the idea "impossible since I'd already met with Frank Sinatra and talked to him about his costume. The moral consideration never deterred Sam. He went right on as if I'd been affirmative in answer to his question about Brando." In fact, Spiegel had begun a stealthy seduction of Marlon Brando once the brass at United Artists gave him cold hard budgetary figures. They'd pony up $1 million to make a movie starring Brando but only half that for a movie starring Sinatra. So Spiegel romanced Brando with a barrage of phone messages, telegrams, dinners, and invitations to private meetings. Little of this courtship worked on Brando, whose favorite word for Spiegel was the Yiddish term *Schnorrer*, as in *moocher* or *chiseler*. Kazan said, "This was [going on] right after Sinatra and the next thing I knew, I heard Sam was talking with his friend Leo Jaffe [about making the movie] at Columbia Pictures. But it was all secret, and neither Budd nor I knew just what he was doing." Spiegel was always a rogue male playing an angle, hedging a bet. While the elusive Brando was busy being Brando, the producer slipped the script to Montgomery Clift, who was not only Sinatra's *From Here to Eternity* costar but also an acting idol and, occasionally, rival of Brando, who viewed him as the prime example of a serious young actor who made astute film choices such as *Red River*, *The Heiress*, and *A Place in the Sun*. Clift promptly turned down the chance to play Terry Malloy in *Waterfront*.

By July 1953, Kazan still planned the movie around Sinatra when Spiegel announced that politically liberal activist Brando continued to resist the possibility of working with Kazan because of his cooperation with HUAC. He felt "conflicted" and said so. He also ridiculed Kazan as a hypocrite, knowing that the director would need to cooperate with gangsters if he hoped to get approval to shoot on the docks. Kazan recalls, "I bridled and said I didn't want the son of a bitch in the film, he wasn't right for the part anyway, and I was perfectly happy with Frank." Spiegel pressed Schulberg to get the script to Brando's MCA agent, Jay Kanter. Fully attuned both to Brando's capriciousness and his personal convictions, Schulberg secreted colored tabs between the pages of the *Waterfront* script before sending it off. Jay Kanter returned the script; all the tabs were left untouched. Said Kanter, "He was always looking for ways to avoid work," but the agent opined that Brando rejected the project not on the basis of the script or his doubts about the creative alchemy between him and Kazan. Kanter confirmed that his highly principled client remained in a period of feeling "very badly" about Kazan's naming names during the HUAC hearings. Privately, he complained about former friends who crossed the street if they saw him coming, assailed him with scornful diatribes, or worse, froze him out completely. Did he expect a tickertape parade? In his autobiography *A Life*, Kazan is voluble on the shame, self-loathing, and recriminations he went through before deciding to name names—a decision he called "disastrous" even though he remained righteous and defiant about his decision for the rest of his life. When Brando wrote of the blacklist in his 1994 autobiography, he spoke passionately of friends of his who "had been deeply hurt. It was especially stupid because most of the people named were no longer Communists." Brando's rejection of the role and the project reached Kazan while Spiegel and Schulberg were with him at his home. With Brando apparently out, the men dug deeper.

Kazan in late July 1953 wrote Budd Schulberg:

> I'm not insane about Brando for this. In fact in my opinion he is quite wrong. But he's a fine actor and if he's really excited about it and will work like a beginner trying to get a start, he can be fine. . . . At any rate he arrives in town Sunday the second of August and leaves on the fifth, and it is imperative repeat imperative that he read the script and give us his yes or no. He cannot take the script to Europe with him. Our time is running short and we cannot wait for his majesty to get comfy in Paris and send us an answer when he feels like it.

This and other correspondence from Kazan indicate his conviction that any trace of the lean and hungry newcomer Brando was fading fast. After all, Kazan had observed firsthand how Brando's joyful spontaneity during the rehearsals and multicity pre-Broadway tryouts for *A Streetcar Named Desire* congealed once the show opened on Broadway to rapturous reviews and stunned audience response. To Kazan and to Brando's costars, when he didn't seem bratty, show-offy, and undisciplined, he seemed indifferent. Rather than prepare before a performance as the other actors did, he'd simply stand in the wings and charge onto the stage as if eager to get the whole damn thing over with. He'd say his lines differently and used different cadences during every performance, sometimes indulging in long silences, throwing his costars curveballs, especially seasoned pro Jessica Tandy, who performed her role in a consistent style at every performance. "He terrified everyone; a talent of that size will do that," said Kazan when commenting on his costars Jessica Tandy and Vivien Leigh from the film version of *Streetcar*. At some performances, Brando would mutter under his breath as the actors playing the doctor and nurse escort Blanche Dubois to the psychiatric hospital: "It's about time they got that lunatic out of here. . . . Thank God, now we can pull down the damn curtain and we can go home." Tandy, at her wit's end, wrote him a schoolmarm-style, very Blanche Dubois letter advising him to improve his diction and treat his colleagues in a more professional manner. Kazan had heard what Brando had been complaining about to his friends, that he practically had to drag himself to the theater nightly "to rape Jessica Tandy." The actor shared a dressing room with Karl Malden, at one point hiring a violinist to serenade them as they donned their *Streetcar* costumes in what Malden described as a highly emotive "gypsy manner." Brando complained to Malden, "This is all child's play. What the hell are we doing? This isn't man's work." His name and image were splashed across theater marquees and magazine pages, critics and audiences praised his talents to the skies, and he stole the show outright from the baffled, supremely professional Tandy. Kazan told Schulberg that Brando appeared to have lost whatever hunger and excitement for performing he once had. He topped national polls of young people who voted him their favorite actor. Meanwhile, critics who responded to his idiosyncratic, often explosive acting style and presence, were already acclaiming him one of the greatest actors of all time. Overnight, the acting styles of such classically trained giants as Olivier and Gielgud seemed obsolete. But Brando came to despise what he viewed as overpraise. He considered himself a trivial talent in a trivial occupation.

What he did not despise was his salary. He began telling reporters, "I became an actor because it's the easiest way I know to make money." When Brando did *Streetcar*, he was making $500 per week and professed indifference to money. By the time of *Waterfront*, he'd become a highly paid film star thanks to *The Men*, the *Streetcar* film, *Viva Zapata!*, *Julius Caesar*, and *The Wild One*, although only one (*Streetcar*) was a sizable hit. In those days, he was earning today's equivalent of $4 million yearly, "more money than I know what to do with," as he told on-and-off girlfriend Ellen Adler, daughter of Stella Adler, the legendary acting coach who taught Method acting to a new generation. Ellen Adler thought he had become "a bit full of himself" at that time. And so Brando dutifully sent most of the money to his parents to manage and invest, which financed their purchase of a Nebraska cattle ranch as a tax shelter. What the money didn't buy was his father's respect or acknowledgment of his rising fame and power. Brando said his father, "who measured everything by money . . . was dumbfounded that I was making more in six months than he made in ten years." Film producers and studio bosses now waited in line until Brando was good and ready. That boy who was rejected by his father and told by academics that he possessed an inferior IQ? He now knew that the world was his. And he made the world *pay*. "He hated this position he had been put in," Ellen Adler said. "He enjoyed the perks, why not? If people were going to be crazy enough to pay him all this money and attention, fine. But they were still crazy." As friend and confidante Maureen Stapleton put it, Brando harbored suspicion that he was "only half as good as people said he was."

In late July 1953, Kazan composed a second letter to Schulberg:

> If we don't get Brando, and I think it most likely we won't, I'm
> for Paul Newman. This boy will definitely be a film star. I have
> absolutely no doubt. He's just as good looking as Brando and his
> masculinity which is strong is also more actual. He's not as good
> an actor as Brando yet, and probably will never be. But he's a
> darn good actor with plenty of power, plenty of insides, plenty
> of sex. He and Malden are working on two scenes to show to
> Sam and yourself. I'm for him without seeing more.

Kazan also wrote to Sam Spiegel about Newman: "He's a really wonderful prospect, handsome, rugged, sexy and somehow turbulent
inside. He looks quite a lot like Brando."

Spiegel, Brando's champion from the outset, thought Brando's
resistance toward Kazan and the project might be weakening. He
urged Kazan to personally reach out to the actor for the sake of the
movie and the prospect of a bigger budget. And so, in late July 1953,
Kazan wrote to Brando:

> I can't pretend that it's easy or simple to write you. Ultimately,
> in our little world, everyone hears everything. I will always feel
> most warmly and devotedly for you, but this does not blot out
> the things unsaid between us. I will for the time leave them
> unsaid. I will write you here professionally, and you can behave
> as you wish from whatever criteria you wish to act from. That's
> your business and even your problem. I'm sending you the
> script of a movie in a state of preparation. I'm very, very hope-
> ful of the script. I've worked very hard on it, and I'm going to
> do a lot more work on it. But you're a sensitive person and you
> will realize it's not finished; you will sense its intention and the
> hope involved in it. It's yet not realized, though it's a great deal

closer than what you read before. It's meant very seriously. It is taken from living people, though distilled and compacted. The problem which it mirrors still exists and the moral problem it treats—the social responsibility of a citizen as it comes into conflict with his personal allegiances—is one of the oldest and most universal of all problems a man can face. My own point of view towards this problem and Budd's too, is clearly set forth. But the script is more of an involvement in the problem than an exhortation of any kind. Make no mistake about it, there is a parallel inference to be drawn to the Inquiries into Communist Activities. This parallelism is not the main value of the script. This is the story of a human in torment, and in danger. The first thing I would do if you did become interested would be to take you over [to] Hoboken and introduce you to Tony Mike DeVincenzo who went through exactly what our Terry goes through. This is a confrontation which would put flesh and blood on the issue on which our script is built. I've spent three evenings with him and it's like being in the presence of a denizen of Dante's *Purgatorio* and finally with him and with the whole waterfront of New York Harbor, the issue is not decided, and will probably be in the process of being decided as we shoot the picture.

I don't want to say more about the picture's theme. Just one word about the part. By the common measure which producers and directors use for casting, you are not right for this part. But you weren't right for the Williams Play [*A Streetcar Named Desire*] either and you weren't right for *Zapata*. This boy is a former fighter, half pure, half hoodlum. He is a boy who has lost his sense of inner dignity or self-worth. At the beginning of our story he doesn't know when he lost it or how. He only discovers that he is behaving like a hoodlum and he has been a contributor to a murder. Slowly thru the unfolding of the incidents of the story and thru his relationship with a girl he discovers the shameful estate to which he has sunken. The body of the story has to do with his effort to find his own dignity and self-esteem once more. He's a boy who suffers at the slightest introspection or self-examination. He goes thru hell. Finally he acts to make himself respect himself, first putting his life in danger and secondly even going out to meet a violent end, so that he will re-establish himself in the sight of his own inner eye. With this "inside," there is a jaunty exterior which is the pathetic remnant of a career where he was once the white-haired boy of the neighborhood, etc. There's much more to say, but you can go on from here, if you care to. I think it's a giant of a part and a tremendous challenge.

Brando's intransigence and unpredictability worried Kazan even more than Sinatra's limited availability. Anyway, he believed he believed he had a fresher, more revelatory candidate in Paul Newman, who was not only hungrier but also available. Besides, he had other pressing matters. Aside from his ongoing work on *Waterfront*, he was prepping for the September 30 opening night of Robert Anderson's play *Tea and Sympathy* at the Ethel Barrymore Theater. For help, Kazan turned to Group Theater friend and colleague Karl Malden, whom he cast in 1947 in a small early movie role in the semi-documentary–style crime drama *Boomerang* and as Jessica Tandy's suitor "Mitch" in the Broadway production of *A Streetcar Named Desire*, a role Malden would eventually reprise in the movie version. "Kazan had the gift of being able to see through to an actor's unique vulnerability," said Malden. "With me, I always felt that he knew how basically insecure I was. What's more, we had come from similar ethnic upbringing, he being of Anatolian Greek descent; so on some level he knew how important my father's approval was to be. As my director, Kazan often became like a father." Kazan was convinced that Malden should become a director and made him his right-hand man. "Since he kept using me," recalled Malden, "I began to realize that he must have seen something in me." Kazan first assigned Malden to cast the other actors around Deborah Kerr in *Tea and Sympathy,* which he did from an office at the Playwrights' Company that he shared temporarily with Kazan's neighbor and recent *Viva Zapata!* and future (*East of Eden*) collaborator John Steinbeck. About this same time, Kazan confided to Malden that he had become intrigued by the great promise he saw in the young stage actor and Actors Studio student Paul Newman.

Though the 28-year-old Newman had yet to appear in a film, Kazan in letters and phone calls to Schulberg in late July 1953, doubled-down on his enthusiasm for the actor's potential for movie stardom, his talent—even his resemblance to Brando. What is more, Kazan signed off on Newman's request to perform his audition for *Waterfront* with Joanne Woodward as his scene partner. Recalls Malden, "[Paul] thought he would have good chemistry with her." Kazan not only agreed with Newman's desire to work with Woodward, his wife-to-be and fellow understudy on Broadway in *Picnic,* having seen her work, he thought she could possibly make a good Edie in the film.

But there was more to Kazan's not "being in love with Brando for this." He had been a hero in Brando's eyes and no longer was. Professionally and personally, Brando no longer turned to him for advice. The bond between them was broken. Besides, Kazan had a credo. If he could find a fresh face—or a fresher one, at least—then he would. He said, "It's my tendency. I don't particularly like stars. If you have Rock Hudson in a picture, you know it's going to turn out well. You know he's not going to be killed in the second reel. Nothing bad can happen. And you also know how the story will turn out. It can only turn out one way. For a story to have the really good qualities of any good story—that is, surprise, unpredictability—it's better to cast fresh people. I also like to work with young actors because they come to work. They come hungry. They're eager to make good. They come every day and they're on time, they're eager and they're looking for something. And then, it's just fun to discover people. I enjoy that."

To show off Newman and Woodward to best advantage, Kazan had Malden rehearse them for a full week in a scene in Ferenc Molnár's 1909 romantic drama *Liliom*. Kazan knew the text intimately, having played the lowlife criminal "Ficzur" in the 1940 Broadway revival starring Burgess Meredith and Ingrid Bergman. The scene prefigures Terry and Edie's dynamic in *Waterfront*, with Newman acting the brutish but magnetic carny and Woodward playing the waifish young woman who is sorry-grateful to have fallen in love with him. Said Karl Malden, "Kazan had phoned and told me that he had to find someone else. Will you do me a favor? I think Paul Newman would be good as the boy. I agreed with Kazan. Newman had a boxer's build and was pretty athletic." The idea, said Malden, was that he would work for a week with Newman and his choice of scene partner, then invite Spiegel to pass judgment. Malden recalled, "We rehearsed for a week. It was beautiful. That's when I first realized that there was something going on there. I couldn't quite put my finger on it, but I think it was the way they'd come to the rehearsal and then leave together, too. All the time I was working on rehearsing the scene with Paul and Joanne, I kept getting phone calls from Marlon's agent Jay Kanter begging me, 'We've got to get Marlon to change his mind.' Mind you, I wasn't even officially cast in the picture at this time, even though Kazan had promised that I'd play the priest. I said to Jay Kanter, 'You're his agent. You know you can never talk Marlon into anything he doesn't want to do.' Anyway, I'd worked on the scene with Paul and Joanne until we all felt they were ready for Spiegel. Paul was so nervous. There was a lot riding on this and so much was at stake for him."

Malden goaded the couple to loosen up for the scene. "Joanne had a kind of innocence and she was damn good. But my concentration was on Paul because he's the one we'd have to sell [to Spiegel]," said Malden. "We'd improv a little and I didn't give him any instructions except to titillate him about Joanne, something very vulgar because that's what the scene is about—is he or isn't he going to lay her in the bushes? She would like it, yet doesn't know what to do about it, and he, being the kind of guy he is, he's for anything at all, anytime! I wanted to give him that freeness. Well, Paul was so excited he couldn't stand still. 'Let me do it! Let me try!,' he said, and the more he did of that, the more I titillated him. Different kinds of sex. Tonight's the night because she won't be here tomorrow. . . . There was a childlike excitement about him, a completely emotional thing that comes from the inside. He just goes all out." Spiegel watched Newman and Woodward play the scene, said, "Good, fine," and off he went.

Good, fine, or not, Kazan remained sold on Newman while Spiegel was obviously stalling for time. Meanwhile, with the single major female role still not cast, the director considered other New York and TV stage actresses as his potential "Edie," including Janice Rule (starring at the time in *Picnic*), Elizabeth Montgomery, and Julie Harris. True to form, Spiegel made end runs around Kazan, offering the role of Edie to the far better known 34-year-old Jennifer Jones and 24-year-old Grace Kelly, who read for Spiegel privately. Of Kelly, who instead made *Rear Window* for Hitchcock, Spiegel said in 1983 that she lost *On the Waterfront* because "she wasn't hungry enough." Then Spiegel, a master of manipulation, released a press announcement that Frank Sinatra had landed the leading role. As if on cue, traveling salesman and abusive father Marlon Brando Sr. contacted agent Jay Kanter. Desperate to get his wayward son back on screen or stage instead of wandering around Europe dodging work, he asked Kanter, "Isn't there anything that you feel he should do?" Brando Sr., having not only read the press about Sinatra's casting but also having heard about Kazan's growing interest in Paul Newman, cannily asked if Sinatra had officially signed to star in *On the Waterfront*. Knowing that this question was coming from the only Brando who mattered, Kanter brokered a meeting between Brando and Sam Spiegel. During their meeting, Spiegel allegedly told Brando, "Politics has nothing to do with this—it's about your talent, it's about your career." Kazan believed that Spiegel manipulated Brando's competitive streak in the matter of Sinatra and Newman. The upshot was that Brando and Jay Kanter held out for a salary of $150,000, a hefty slice of a movie budgeted only between $750,00 to $880,000. Spiegel angled for a drastically lower salary sweetened by the added incentive of a cut of the profits. Kanter stonewalled, and Spiegel agreed to Brando's terms.

It was time to tell Sinatra that the role of a lifetime would not be his. In a meeting attended by Kazan, Spiegel, and Sinatra's agent, Abe Lastfogel, Spiegel blamed Sinatra's limited availability and the movie's tight shooting schedule for the decision to hire Brando. Lastfogel decimated the specious excuse. Said Kazan, "I've never heard so much screaming from a pair of short, fat men. . . . Abe [Lastfogel] had the Eagle flushing crimson, floundering and perspiring and flapping his wings." The agent accused Spiegel of using underhanded tricks to welch on a deal. Actor Karl Malden recalled, "[Sinatra] threatened to show up for work anyway and sue the pants off of Spiegel and the studio if they made him leave." Recalled Kazan, "Sam had conned Marlon into making the film and I let him do the dirty work and said nothing. I wouldn't have done what Sam did but I was glad he did it; it was what I really wanted. I turned my face the other way as S.P. Eagle informed Sinatra's agency, William Morris, that Frank was out. I was silent because, although I liked Frank and was sure I could make the picture with him, I always preferred Brando to anybody" (this despite his insisting otherwise in his private letters).

A second meeting got scheduled. As was Kazan's way, this time, he sent Budd Schulberg to face Sinatra and his agent. Spiegel recalled

Sinatra's being "mad as hell. God, he wanted that part. He screamed at me. He practically came to blows with Spiegel. He had his heart set on [doing the film]. The unfortunate truth is that Sinatra couldn't have done it. He just couldn't act in that way, the way Brando did. But who else could?" Sinatra, not placated, insisted on a consolation prize: he wanted to be cast as Father Barry, a role he saw as his ticket to a Best Supporting Actor Oscar nomination. Without consulting Kazan or Schulberg, Spiegel offered Sinatra the waterfront priest role. And when Kazan and Schulberg insisted Sinatra be denied that plum supporting role, the singer threated to sue Spiegel for $500,000 in damages. The suit was settled out of court, and for years, rumors flew that the producer smoothed things over with Sinatra by gifting him with a world-class painting worth far more than $500,000.

According to Spiegel's biographer, Natasha Fraser-Cavassoni, though, the Sinatra–Spiegel feud played out differently. Initially, Sinatra demanded $100,000 to save face. Instead, the producer would later spend some of his *Waterfront* profits to build Sinatra a state-of-the-art screening room at his main residence. Hearing from friends that Sinatra continually derided him around town, the producer tried again to make amends by sending Sinatra a crate of wildly expensive rare whiskey. Sinatra, still not mollified, tried to provoke an incident at the posh Beverly Hills restaurant Roma-noff's in 1957. Sinatra sat in a booth with two men when into the restaurant swanned Spiegel and his wife and their guests Billy and Audrey Wilder and Rita Hayworth and husband James Hill. As the illustrious group passed Sinatra's table, Spiegel said, "Hey there," and was ushered into the booth immediately adjacent to Sinatra's. The singer turned and offered Spiegel congratulations on the success of his *The Bridge on the River Kwai*. Spiegel thanked him and continued conversing with his guests. Sinatra rose, poked Spiegel's shoulder, and said, "Listen, when you speak to me, it's not 'Hey there.'" When

Sinatra punched the producer's shoulder again, Spiegel stared up at him and said, "You're lucky that I bother to speak to you at all." Tensions rose, and Rita Hayworth (the film siren who had grown to dislike Sinatra while making *Pal Joey* with him) balled her fists and comically said, "Let me at him! Let me at him!" When Sinatra sat back down and shouted, "Hey, fat man," Spiegel grabbed the table's edge, quietly furious; turned to Sinatra's table; and said, "Frank, if you would like to meet me outside without your henchmen, it would be my pleasure." Sinatra's bravado deflated like a pin-pricked balloon.

Kazan attempted to do some fence-mending of his own. He sent a letter to Abe Lastfogel about the Sinatra contretemps on November 2, 1953:

> Obviously from my point of view the decision to go ahead with Frank was a severe compromise. Not on artistic grounds. I was quite happy that way. Frank would have been fine in the part. Brando was my first choice, but since I could not have him and had completely abandoned hope of having him, Frank was a happy choice for me. . . . The alternate to Frank was an unknown boy in the cast of *Picnic* [Newman]. His release was a dubious matter. . . . Then, after Frank was all set, Brando walked in one day, to my complete surprise, and said he wanted to go ahead. I wanted him. Not just Sam. I wanted him. Not that I was unhappy with Frank. But with Brando there would be no time pressure. My guess is that this picture will take 42 days, even possibly a few more. We now have a decent budget. . . . I don't like to get hurt and I hate to hurt anyone. Nor do I feel that the thing was handled well by Sam. Sam says that's the only way he could have done it. I'm not sure it was. One thing is sure: the change was necessary. We had done something desperate in accepting Frank with 27 days, desperate and foolish. It's terrible and regrettable that Frank had to be hurt. But couldn't the hurt be

partially assuaged by having Frank announce that he withdrew because the schedule did not permit. And couldn't another part of his hurt be softened by my writing him and assuring him that the basis of the change with me was time. I had gotten myself in a foolish and desperate (but by me, necessary) spot, and I had to get out of it when I saw a way out. I'm not callous to Frank's feelings. But say this much for us: when we went into it with Frank we went in on complete good faith. In fact our demands were craven. We begged him to give us a few more days. He was unable to, so I got us three more on the phone with Lew. We did not ask him to give up the Fox musical or anything like that. We were beggars. And we begged. But too much work and pain and time from Budd and myself are riding on this thing—to do anything else than what we allowed Sam to do. I wish Sam had done it differently but Abe I want you to know I'm glad right now that we have Marlon. And make no mistake about that.

Kazan delivered on his offer to send Sinatra a letter of apology. Months after receiving that letter, Sinatra answered: "For me to tell you that I was not deeply hurt would not be telling you my true feelings. However with the passing of time and after re-reading your letter, how could I do or say anything other than I, too, want to be friends with you."

Spiegel hounded Kanter to wrangle Brando. Said Kanter, "Of course at the time, people were chasing Marlon to do everything and anything. He was the top of the heap as far as the young stars of that period." Marlon Brando Sr. continually hectored Kanter, concerned about losing his meal ticket—a prodigiously gifted, if capricious son who was only too content to flit-off to Europe and to avoid as many stage and film offers as possible. Of course, this is the same father who subjected his son to unprovoked verbal humiliation and physical abuse from a very young age, never offered a kind word about Brando's theater and film work, and frequently left Marlon's fragile, alcoholic mother and the children penniless while he traveled for work. All Brando Jr. ever hoped to do was gain the approval of a man he recalled as "a card-carrying prick . . . a frightening, brooding, angry, hard-drinking man, a bully who loved to give orders and issued ultimatums. His blood consisted of compounds of alcohol, testosterone, adrenaline and anger."

The story goes that when Kanter mentioned to Brando the waterfront project, Brando stonewalled. But this time, there was a "tell": he asked his agent who was most likely to play Terry Malloy instead. The intensely competitive Brando, of course, knew that Paul Newman had emerged as Kazan's prime contender. Kanter, of course, knew exactly why Brando was asking. Despite Brando's feelings of outrage toward Kazan and his HUAC testimony, he agreed to do the movie. Yes, the role was difficult to resist, and Kazan's emotional investment in the material was obvious and persuasive. But to Brando, other more personally compelling factors came into play. One of them was Spiegel's concession that come hell or high water, Brando could quit work at 4:00 p.m. to be driven from Hoboken to Manhattan for his appointments with psychiatrist Bela Mittelman— Kazan's own therapist. In private, this son of two alcoholics was in disarray, suffering frequent panic attacks, haunted by fears of abandonment, and often so overcome by rage that he feared he might kill someone, as he confessed to Kazan. Did Mittelman influence Brando to reunite with Kazan? He certainly tried to help Brando let go of old anger, resentments, and psychic scars. Similarly, Stella Adler, Brando's highly influential acting coach, life mentor, and intimate friend, and her spouse, the renowned theater director and drama critic Harold Clurman, told Brando they had chosen to forgive Kazan but never forget what he did. Karl Malden believed that Brando's insistence on seeing his psychiatrist during the workweek was not only a survival tool but also a means of reminding Kazan that Brando was in charge. It was also a signal to those who reviled

Kazan that Brando would not let him off the hook for betraying old friends and colleagues. In fact, Kazan wrote Brando many years later: "I remember on *Waterfront* where you told me repeatedly while we were shooting the picture that you weren't enthusiastic about it and were only making the picture 'because you wanted to pay for your psychiatrist and to stay in the city.'"

Yet even Schulberg, who had also begun to warm to the notion of Paul Newman as Terry Malloy, also expressed concerns to Kazan about Brando. Schulberg said, "I thought Brando needed to be around real fighters, maybe have them to come in and show him the ropes— hear the language, the ways boxers talk, how they move outside and inside the ring, how they walk, how they fight." Kazan and Brando agreed. Schulberg, a rabid boxing fan who served as the first boxing editor for *Sports Illustrated* in the 1950s, handpicked retired young middleweight Roger Donaghue to meet and work with Brando at the legendary Stillman's Gym on 54th Street and 8th Avenue in midtown Manhattan. Donaghue, formerly known as "The Golden Boy" (the inspiration for the screenplay's earlier title *The Golden Warrior*), had emerged victorious from 25 out of 27 of his bouts. But his ascent ended on August 29, 1951, in Madison Square Garden on 8th Avenue and 39th Street when the 20-year-old Donaghue's left hook knocked 19-year-old George Flores unconscious during the eighth round. Donaghue waited at the hospital throughout Flores's brain surgery, but Flores died several days later. Donaghue donated his winnings from the fight and his next bout to his opponent's widow and her infant. The event marked Donaghue for life. He quit boxing and became a beer salesman, making fast friends with bandleader Guy Lombardo and Schulberg not long after his fateful fall from grace. It was from Donaghue that Schulberg first heard five words that would go on to become part of film history. When the writer asked, "If things had gone a different way at Madison Square Garden that night, could you have been a champion?" Donaghue answered:

"I could have been a contender." Donaghue, who also impressed Kazan for being "softspoken and rather cultured" and "a born raconteur," thought he was so good a boxing coach and a stabilizing influence on Brando that he kept him on throughout the production and put him on camera along with the other former prizefighters handpicked by Schulberg, including heavyweights, Tony "Two Ton" Galento, Abe Simon, and Tami Mauriello.

## The Men

Before Kazan tapped Rod Steiger to play "Charley Malloy," the mobbed-up, morally compromised older brother of the leading character, the Actors Studio devotee had appeared in such Broadway productions as Arthur Miller's adaptation of Ibsen's *An Enemy of the People* and an Orson Welles–written adaptation of Herman Melville's *Moby Dick*. Steiger had also done considerable television work but had appeared in one previous film, *Teresa*, the sensitive Fred Zinnemann–directed, Stewart Stern–written film about an Italian war bride and her young GI husband. The volatile, compelling, and underused 28-year-old Steiger, son of a vaudevillian who abandoned him and an alcoholic mother, was exactly the kind of actor with whom Kazan wanted to work. Aside from observing Steiger at the Actors Studio, Kazan was especially impressed by his heartbreaking portrayal of a lonely, lovelorn Bronx butcher in Paddy Chayefsky's acclaimed *Marty*, broadcast in May 1953 on the *Philco Playhouse*. Producers Burt Lancaster and Harold Hecht invited Steiger to repeat his starring role in the 1955 movie version, but Ernest Borgnine played Marty instead when Steiger refused to sign a multifilm contract. The *On the Waterfront* offer came at just the right time. Said Steiger:

> Elia Kazan said to me, "Will you go to Budd Schulberg—he wrote a script called *On the Waterfront*? You read the taxi scene

with him and if he likes you, then you can play Marlon Brando's brother." Well, I almost fell on the floor because we all saw Marlon Brando doing a magnificent performance in *A Streetcar Named Desire* and my god, this is some colleague to work with. I went and read with Schulberg which was difficult because he stuttered. This is an acting thing—when you work with somebody after the second day, if they're terrible or they have a quirk or something you're not used to, you must convince yourself that's part of the character. If you don't, every time they do this odd thing of theirs, your concentration's going to go. It takes you a couple of years to go, *OK, that's part of the character.* Anyway, we went and did it. I was a nervous wreck. But we did it, I was pleased. And the rest is more or less history.

But much of Steiger's pleasure would fade once he worked opposite Brando on their most crucial scene.

Kazan's casting of Lee J. Cobb as the ironically nicknamed "Johnny Friendly," the rapacious power-mad union boss, was loaded with social and political resonance. He and Kazan went a long way back. They had acted together in the groundbreaking 1935 Group Theater Broadway production of *Waiting for Lefty* and in the 1937 Broadway debut of *Golden Boy*. When Kazan was casting his legendary production of Arthur Miller's *Death of a Salesman*, Cobb won the role over such other contenders as James Cagney (Miller's choice), Walter Huston, Roman Bohnen (the presumed front-runner), and Fredric March, the latter being Kazan's first choice who declined because right-wingers were eyeing his liberal political leanings as closely as they were Kazan's and Miller's. Both men had also named names to HUAC. Kazan said of his and Cobb's relationship, which "started close" but "thinned out, "I knew him for a mass of contradictions: loving and hateful, anxious yet still supremely pleased with himself, smug but full of doubt, guilty and arrogant, fiercely competitive but very withdrawn, publicly private, suspicious but always reaching for trust, boastful with a modest air, begging for total acceptance no matter what he did to others. In other words, the part was him." In other words, Kazan somehow failed to see aspects of himself in Cobb but recognized the actor's rightness for Willy Loman. But their professional relationship went south when Cobb—who received critical hosannahs for his performance—began milking the role; slowing down the pace mercilessly on stage; and sinking into deep, public depression when not onstage. Kazan and Miller were enraged by what Cobb's showboating did to their play. Still, six years after the play, Arthur Miller called Cobb "the greatest actor I ever saw, when he was creating the role of Willy Loman in *Death of a Salesman*."

Karl Malden spent 11 days with Father John Corridan, the real-life inspiration for his "Father Barry" character. Said Malden, who would commute daily from the two-bedroom apartment in Peter Cooper Village on Manhattan's East Side that he shared with his wife Mona and daughters Mila and Carla, "[Father Corridan] was a compelling character. He himself begged me, 'Karl don't play me like a priest. Play me like a man. I was born in this neighborhood. When I was growing up there were two ways to go. Become a priest or a hood.'" Malden told Kazan that he wanted to play his character as a man who had become a priest but had the personality of a hood; he also wanted to use an undercurrent of Corridan's pervasive sense of residual guilt over an incident that had inspired Budd Schulberg to write the script in the first place. Recalled Malden, who had toiled as a steelworker before becoming an actor:

> When a longshoreman had been refused a chip [the little tag that permits you to go to work that day], Father John had advised him that this was a violation of the law and that he should go ahead and work anyway. The longshoreman did that and, within a day, was beaten up and thrown into the river for dead.

Miraculously, the man survived, but that night, while Father John was waiting to learn of his condition, he stayed up all night walking through Central Park mulling over what his advice had caused to happen. The next morning he walked back, stood on a box on the decks, and delivered the sermon that became an inspiration for *On the Waterfront*.

Kazan filled out the supporting cast with some of the most authentic and interesting actors in the business, including Martin Balsam, Fred Gwynne, Nehemiah Persoff, Michael V. Gazzo, and Pat Hingle.

## *"A Fresh-Faced, Sensitive Young Irish Girl . . . a Fruitcake": Finding Edie*

Once they had landed Brando, Kazan filled in the cast with Actors Studio familiars. But casting the film's sole major female role went all the way down to the wire. The character was written as an almost angelic, impassioned Catholic school–reared young woman perhaps as young as 19 but not more than in her early 20s. Kazan found that finding the right young woman was a tricky business. Recalls Karl Malden:

> One afternoon, Kazan and I were walking from The Playwrights' Company to the Actors Studio for an afternoon session when he mentioned to me that he was having a helluva time casting that part. I was already familiar with the script and I knew that the essence of the part was that this girl be different from everyone else in that tough neighborhood. She has spent her life in Catholic schools distanced from the waterfront experience. I remembered a girl with whom I had done a scene at the Studio. Even her name was perfect: Eva Marie Saint. I mentioned her to Gadg but he had never seen her.

Kazan, however, asserted that although he had seen Saint, he retained only a vague recollection of her work in Actors Studio classes. Budd Schulberg claimed that he and Kazan "thumbed through the entire *Players' Guide* and finally came to Eva Marie Saint." Let's stick with the more plausible-sounding version supplied by Malden, who said that a week after he mentioned Saint, Kazan asked him to begin rehearsing scenes with her as well as with a second actress. That second actress was the up-and-coming daughter of film star Robert Montgomery, the gifted Elizabeth Montgomery, who was then appearing on Broadway alongside Arlene Francis and Cliff Robertson in the light romantic comedy *Late Love*.

Kazan, still on the fence about Montgomery, had sought out Eva Marie Saint one early November evening at Henry Miller's Theater (now the Stephen Sondheim Theater) on West 43rd Street. She was appearing in Horton Foote's *The Trip to Bountiful*. The play had debuted on NBC television on March 1, 1953, before it, along with Gish and Saint, transferred to Broadway and garnered Saint a Theatre World Award. Her cool and ladylike presence, angelic with an intriguing undercurrent of sensuality, impressed Kazan, a remarkable feat considering she was acting opposite Lillian Gish, of whom Brooks Atkinson in his *New York Times* review wrote, "Everything being possible, Lillian Gish may someday give a finer performance than her Mrs. Carrie Watts in *The Trip to Bountiful*. But no one has a right ever to expect anything finer. For this is Miss Gish's masterpiece." But the show's director, Fred Coe, had unstinting praise for Saint, too, citing her rare "ability to transmit inner purity." That was something Kazan and Schulberg were looking for in their search for the right actress to play Edie Doyle. Explains Schulberg, "We'd looked at easily three hundred girls on either coast and we were awfully discouraged. It was a risky part. The girl had to be able to play a convent girl to set the plot in motion. But later she had to be able to show a passion that could convincingly come from a slum background." Kazan sent Sam Spiegel and Schulberg to see *The Trip to Bountiful*. Schulberg thought she "had a really lovely quality." After the show, he told her about the involvement of Kazan and Brando, and he and Spiegel set up a meeting with Kazan the following day. Despite her serious reservations about the movie business and how it treats women, she reasoned, while talking with her TV director husband, Jeffrey Hayden, *After all, this is Kazan, this is Brando*. She accepted the invitation and agreed to work on scenes from the script with her friend and colleague Karl Malden before facing Brando.

"I'm sure I knew every blonde actress in New York who had been reading for that role," said Saint, who was 29 at the time of *On the Waterfront* and an emerging television actress dubbed by one smitten critic "the Helen Hayes of television." Among her many live TV appearances in such anthology series as *Suspense* and *The Actor's Studio*, she had also starred for over two years on *One Man's Family*, the TV version of the long-running radio series about a tightly knit San Francisco family. Although Saint learned that Elizabeth Montgomery was among the many fair-haired young actresses who had been reading for the role, it is unclear whether she knew that Malden worked with one by day and the other in the afternoon. Says Malden, "[It was] maybe just three or four days when, out of the blue, Kazan told me to forget it. He had made up his mind. I understood and concurred with his choice. Eva looked like a girl raised by nuns, a girl who had been protected from the raw side of life. Liz Montgomery, also a fine actress, looked exactly like what she was: a girl from Beverly Hills with the confidence that came from the prep school education she actually had." Kazan responded to Saint's immediacy, her almost preternatural calm, her otherworldliness. She told him and others that her work in live television had helped enormously. "It's all concentration," she said. "With the million and one things happening during a television program—three cameras on you simultaneously, electricians rushing around hellbent, everyone calling to everyone else—you *must* concentrate. Television is a wonderful teacher because it forces you to be undistracted." Undistracted but realistic, Saint harbored doubts that the *Waterfront* role would go to her.

Grounded and refreshingly "un-actressy," Saint seemed almost destined to play such a role. Born in Newark, New Jersey, to schoolteacher mother, Eva Marie (née Rice) Saint, and a Quaker father, John Merle Saint, an executive for the B. F. Goodrich Company, she recalled a stable, secure homelife for herself and her older sister, Adelaide: "I had good parents who made for my sister and me a beautiful, loving childhood. We were living through the Depression but we never knew we were in one. My mother made everything we wore. We ate canned beans and I didn't like them—still don't—but my parents made for us a wonderful home in Queens." Often describing her young self as shy, withdrawn, and lacking confidence, she'd followed in the footsteps of her sister (who became a research chemist) by attending Bowling Green State University in Ohio thinking she would become a teacher like her mother. Success in college plays and radio shows persuaded her to switch her major to speech, and on graduating in 1946, she got her parents' OK to become a professional actress, continuing to live at home now that they had moved to Long Island. She did many commercials and some modeling jobs and met unsuccessfully with countless theater producers and directors until in 1947, director Joshua Logan cast her in the sole female role in Broadway's soon-to-be-blockbuster military comedy drama *Mister Roberts*. But he promptly fired her for looking too young and innocent and replaced her with Jocelyn Brando (Marlon's sister, how's that for irony?) but later hired her back as Jocelyn Brando's understudy. She was already married to budding director Jeffrey Hayden, and at his suggestion, had spent two highly productive years in five-times-a-week psychiatric therapy when *On the Waterfront* came along. She said, "I knew of it but, before Elia Kazan approached me, I didn't try out for it because I was in the theater and doing live television. I had made the rounds once for films and they asked me my bust size, my height, weight, and all of that. I thought, 'I'm not studying with Lee Strasberg at the Actors Studio to be asked those questions. This is silly. This is not for me.' So, I never went back and made the rounds again. I wanted to stay in the theater and had no desire to make films." Nowhere in the film community would Saint or her fellow members of the Actors Studio in New York—such as Karl Malden, Rod Steiger, Lee J. Cobb, and Kazan himself, who cofounded the studio in 1947—take anything even approaching the equivalent of Kazan's commitment pledge, "The Actors' Vow":

> I will admit rejection, admit pain,
> Admit frustration, admit even pettiness,
> Admit shame, admit outrage,
> Admit anything and everything
> That happens to me.

It's almost axiomatic to say that the Actors Studio—where Saint had been studying regularly since 1948—changed overnight our perception of great acting, especially in film. It brought to us a different sense of truth, naturalism, and freedom and privileged moments of what Elia Kazan labeled "a final intimacy." Before Brando, there was John Garfield and Montgomery Clift—though, before them, it must be noted that such stars as James Cagney and James Stewart had unerring gifts for naturalism. In the wake of Brando, though, came a wave of semi-forgotten 1960s-era would-be Brandos, such as Christopher Jones, Michael Parks, and a young Burt Reynolds. Those actors presaged a second-wave generation of 1970s trailblazers, including Al Pacino, Dustin Hoffman, John Cazale, Robert

Duvall, and Jessica Lange and, today, Oscar Isaac, Jessica Chastain, Adam Driver, Paul Mescal, and more. The Studio not only brought a new standard of truth but also a new standard of beauty and sensuality. For Eva Marie Saint in the 1950s, the training was a salvation. She says:

> I was very shy and I had to break through that. I couldn't have done it on my own. Maybe I wouldn't have done it with another teacher, but Lee Strasberg was *the* person. Here's one of my favorite stories about Lee. I had been doing some print modeling and that led to my doing some TV modeling. I wasn't a great model. I smiled too much. I showed emotion when the best models show nothing in their face and that's why they're so successful. I could not do that. But one time, with Lee, I had just finished doing these scenes by beautiful authors and when the session was up, I said, "Oh, Lee, I'm so depressed. Now, I have to do an Admiral TV commercial after doing this beautiful work . . ." He just stopped me and said, "Eva Marie, do you like to eat? Do you like to pay your rent? Just go do your job, please." So, I went to my job at Radio City to do this commercial for Admiral television sets. It was live TV, of course, as was done in the '50s. As part of this commercial, there were two antennas on either side of the television and part of my job was to actually say to the television audience, "Now, ladies, this is so easy, even a woman can do it!" I said it through gritted teeth. I pulled up the antenna to show how easy it was then I went to the other side. But when I pulled it, it didn't go up so they had to go to black. I got fired, the only time I was ever fired. I never did another commercial.

But at least she didn't smile too much.

For her *Waterfront* audition, Saint recalls Kazan's putting Brando and her together in a room with barely an introduction.

"He didn't take his eyes off us," she said of the director who "took me aside and, to set up our improvisation, told me, 'Now, Eva Marie, you have a sister who isn't at home but she has a boyfriend she's been dating and this boyfriend is coming to visit her. Your father's against it because this boy's wanted by the cops, your father says he'll turn the boy in. You are alone. You're not accustomed to being with a young man. You're a religious girl but there's something about the boy that appeals to you. Your action is to not let him in the house under any circumstances.'" I don't know what Kazan told Marlon. All I know is that Marlon got in that door. He put on the radio. We started dancing and he did something to flip my skirt. It was too much. It was *all too* much and I remember crying a little afterward. But Kazan, in his genius, saw the chemistry and how it could work for the movie.

Spiegel and Schulberg also watched how the two actors set off sparks. Says Saint, "The charm, the smile, he was beautiful then. He was just so attractive. All I know is that I ended up crying. Crying and laughing. I mean there was so much attraction there . . . [t]hat smile of his. I mean, I can see it in my mind's eye to this day. I was not frightened. He wasn't mean. He was very tender and funny." From Budd Schulberg, "[Marlon] was experienced, she was nervous and when they began to improvise this scene around Kazan's story, I turned to Sam Spiegel and said, What do they need a writer for?"

Soon after, Kazan told Saint that the role was hers. Still disbelieving, unsure, and resistant to moviemaking, Saint laid out her concerns to Jeffrey Hayden, who was nothing but encouraging. Despite her misgivings, she decided to accept the challenge. She said:

I wasn't even fully aware of the entirety of the story. The first day of shooting, I remember leaving our Greenwich Village apartment at 26 W. 9th Street with tears running down my face. I was so nervous. Before I left, Jeffrey grabbed my hand and said, "Now, listen, honey, don't worry. You're from the Actors Studio. Elia Kazan is directing it and you're in his hands. Your friend Karl Malden is in it, Rod Steiger—all your friends from the Actors Studio." I stopped crying. So in the daytime, I would take the subway to the location in Hoboken. After a day of filming, I would go home, cook dinner for my dear husband and then go to the theater to do *The Trip to Bountiful*. I did what I had to do and after the play closed in early December, then I was able to complete the scenes for *On the Waterfront* at night.

"Marlon Brando had put me off balance right then and there in that audition," she said. It could be said that Brando would keep her—and other *Waterfront* team members—off balance throughout the entire filming. And if she had not been so deeply in love with her husband, let alone so centered and sensible, she might have even tumbled for her magnetic, complicated costar. Nothing like that happened, however.

*Whenever penny-pinching producer Sam Speigel alighted from his limo and swooped onto the set, reeking of expensive cologne and chateaubriand, he drove the underpaid, overworked, miserable cast and crew closer to mutiny. But, without Speigel, Kazan admitted,* On the Waterfront *would not have been made.* PHOTOFEST

*Brando rode the train to Hoboken daily in his costume and spent time with the dockworkers hired as extras, who accepted him as one of their own.* COLUMBIA PICTURES/PHOTOFEST © COLUMBIA PICTURES

*Elia Kazan allowed Brando to apply his own makeup, which grew progressively more theatrically baroque as the director exalted his informer character toward saintly martyrdom.* COLUMBIA PICTURES/PHOTOFEST © COLUMBIA PICTURES

*The set visit of Brando's parents, the alcoholic, unloving Marlon Brando Sr. and the beloved alcoholic depressive Dodie, sent the actor into a tailspin.* COLUMBIA PICTURES/PHOTOFEST © COLUMBIA PICTURES

*"The charm, the smile, he was beautiful then. He was just so attractive. That smile of his. I can see it in my mind's eye to this day," Eva Marie Saint said of her costar.* COLUMBIA PICTURES/PHOTOFEST © COLUMBIA PICTURES

*Host Thelma Ritter looks on while Elia Kazan steps up to accept his Best Director Oscar for* On the Waterfront. PHOTOFEST

*Despite its status as a landmark in American cinema, the taxicab scene aroused Brando's disdain and behavior toward Rod Steiger that launched a lifelong feud.* COLUMBIA PICTURES/
PHOTOFEST © COLUMBIA PICTURES

*Movie magic combined Elysian Park (Hudson Street between 10th and 11th), Stevens Park (Hudson Street), and Church Square Park (400 Garden Street) as backdrop for Brando's iconic improvised "glove scene" moment that, says Saint "shows the genius of Marlon Brando. I'm convinced that, in rehearsal, any other actor would have picked up the glove and handed it to me."* AUTHOR'S COLLECTION

*When Brando and Eva Marie Saint filmed the truck chase scene in Court Street, a narrow cobbled alleyway in Hoboken, New Jersey, the truck driver came at them too fast, forcing Brando to smash open a door that was supposed to be unlocked to provide an escape, cutting his hand.* COLUMBIA PICTURES/PHOTOFEST © COLUMBIA PICTURES

*Kazan and company filmed the explosive Waterfront Commission courtroom scene in the cramped quarters of the Hoboken City Hall.* COLUMBIA PICTURES/PHOTOFEST © COLUMBIA PICTURES

On the Waterfront's *Oscar-winning screenwriter Bud Schulberg, like director Elia Kazan, named names during the HUAC hearings.* COLUMBIA PICTURES/PHOTOFEST © COLUMBIA PICTURES

# FIVE

# Production

## *Clash of the Titans*

With the casting and production details finally gelling, Sam Spiegel's strengths and weaknesses came to the fore. Said Kazan, "Sam was by far the canniest negotiator I've ever known. On every issue we negotiated on this picture . . . he got the better of me—and my lawyers. . . . He charmed you as he cheated you." Although, by the literal terms of the contract, Kazan owned 25 percent of the film, the director admitted, "I never knew what the hell [Spiegel] was doing with *Waterfront.*" Their firm start date looming, Spiegel—who, after all, had the screenplay read to him in bed and appeared only mildly interested in producing the film to begin with—suddenly began acting like a man obsessed, exhibiting autocratic and intrusive tendencies that would soon make him about as beloved to the crew and filmmakers as Captain Bligh. While Spiegel treated Marlon Brando like a golden boy—or golden warrior, rather—Schulberg and Kazan bore the brunt of the producer's mania for micromanagement.

This led to an immediate and volatile clash with Kazan about how roughed-up Brando should be made to look in his role as a former boxer. Kazan wanted to push for realism and lobbied for "toughening up" the actor's good looks and confining him to two changes of costume. He discussed some bold changes with makeup artists Fred Ryle and Bill Herman, including the possibility of fitting Brando with prosthetic putty appliances to suggest a battered nose, lowered brows, and scarred drooping eyelids. With costumer Anna Hill Johnstone, he and Budd Schulberg explored typical work clothing worn by longshoremen. Spiegel, with his eyes firmly on Brando's appeal as a sex symbol, considered some of Kazan's ideas extreme and, from a box-office perspective, almost self-defeating. He brought up how Brando's costuming by Lucinda Ballard in *A Streetcar Named Desire* was based on the designer's observation of Con Ed workers in the wild, wearing clothes so dirty and sweat soaked that "they had stuck to their bodies." But to achieve that look, Ballard had bought T-shirts, then dyed and washed them repeatedly so they shrank to accent his torso. She had a tailor taper and cut Brando's blue jeans until they clung to every muscle. He made a T-shirt and jeans a symbol of fuck-all American cool. That's what Spiegel wanted for Brando as Terry. When he and Kazan could no longer discuss the subject without erupting into another of their public shouting matches, Spiegel gave up on the costuming and focused on Brando's face. He resorted to a series of memos, one of which read: "One of the most perfect things about Marlon is his nose and let's not deliberately go out of our way to mar it. . . . I would greatly appreciate it if you would agree with me on this issue as it may eliminate great regrets later." Said Spiegel's wife Betty, "Sam was extremely fond of Marlon, even protective. Sam understood that part of Marlon's appeal to audiences came from his looks and physicality. Sam believed that Brando not looking like Brando in *Viva Zapata!* had turned-off audiences and he was afraid that Kazan and Marlon might step right into the same trap twice. Who'd want to disguise a face like that?"

One obvious answer is, of course, Brando himself, whom film critic and film historian David Thomson described in *Waterfront* as "beautiful as anyone had been on screen—so he labored to seem authentic or ordinary. He refined Terry's humbleness, like an actress grooming herself in a mirror." In the end, Kazan and Brando met Spiegel in the middle. Brando was given almost free rein to apply his own makeup, as he had done for his stage roles. In the end, Brando's Terry still looked like Brando but one with swollen ears and eyelids, and brows emulating scar tissue damage. At times, he looked properly battered and beaten down by his days as a fighter. In other moments, though, his makeup might have looked better viewed from fifth row center at a Broadway theater than on a 40-foot movie theater screen. That said, the makeup trickery that gave Brando the look of a slit right eyebrow worked well. The thick, perfectly shaped brows, black eyeliner, and bulging latex bruises Brando dons for the film's last 20 minutes are distractingly theatrical. As for his costuming, Kazan and costumer Anna Hill Johnstone came up with solutions even Sam Spiegel liked. The first was the red-and-black Buffalo plaid wool jacket Brando wears through most of the picture. It was an apt choice because Brando made it look cool while still being entirely authentic, and Sears was among the sellers of affordable versions of the jacket in the 1940s and 1950s. (Today, the handmade replica version of the now-iconic jacket, the "Aero Waterfront," costs over $600). The second was the solid-color wool bomber jacket with shearling collar. Again, the star and movie made the jacket so iconic that custom replicas from The Real McCoy's and Bench & Loom cost $700 and up today.

For all of Kazan's complaints about Spiegel's creative meddling, piratical nature, and underhandedness, he remained unshakable in his praise of the producer's "instinctive story sense," which demanded constant reexamination, deconstruction, and revising of the screenplay right up to the first day of production. Without it, "our film would have been a failure," Kazan said. Any time Kazan and Schulberg thought they finally had a viable shooting script in hand, the producer would infuriate them by saying, "Let's open it up again." Spiegel was variously called "a taskmaster," "a bear for structure," and "maddeningly manipulative." He required Schulberg to endlessly rethink, revise, and finesse his work. For no apparent reasons other than budgetary, Spiegel carped about Schulberg's script being over-long and meandering—and he did so daily during the story confer-ences he convened with Kazan and Schulberg in the sitting room of his suite at the St. Regis Hotel in Manhattan. (Once, when Kazan spotted atop Spiegel's desk bureau thick rolls of American Express checks, he was only half-joking when he wondered aloud whether Spiegel was "a flight risk.") Although Schulberg agreed with some of Spiegel's notes for improving the screenplay, the process of con-stant deconstruction and rebuilding wore on him. He also began to suspect some sort of conspiracy between his director and producer. Otherwise, why did he often find Spiegel and Kazan whispering con-spiratorially when he'd return to the hotel suite from the bathroom? Schulberg reached a breaking point. "After about the eighth or ninth time, I blew up. *What the fuck are you two guys whispering about? What secret can you possibly have that you don't want me to know about? This thing is part of me, I am starving with it, struggling with it.*" Finally letting loose with what he'd clearly been tamping down, he came clean about his discontent, adding, "I've been on this god-dam project for two years. I've taken practically nothing up front. I'm gambling like you on a percentage of the profits. It's beginning to break me. I've had to mortgage my farm. Sam hasn't even paid me the lousy five thousand dollars he's owed me for months. I've written my heart out on this goddam thing. So what the hell can you two bastards be whispering about?"

Kazan said:

> Sam is what drove Schulberg crazy. He said, "Let's open it up again. Let's open it up again. Let's reexamine it. Let's see if we've got it right." And he worked on that script thinning it down and tightening it up. Budd was great. He never stopped, and between them, they worked like hell, although I think they had

a lot of antagonism. Budd was living in the country in Pennsylvania and one night his wife woke up about 3:30 in the morning and looked in the bathroom and Budd was shaving. She said, "Budd, what the hell are you doing shaving for at 3:30 in the morning?" He said, "I'm going to New York." "What are you going to New York for?" He said, "I'm going to New York to kill Sam Spiegel." He was that mad at him. He did go to New York but he never killed Sam Spiegel.

Over the decades, the incident gained the reputation of being a jest. But Schulberg in his later years admitted his animosity toward Spiegel: "I really wanted to murder him. I seriously considered it. I am not proud of it." Even Kazan would write in his autobiography, "Everything was cool between me and S.P. until I began to work with him. Then I got to see his other side and I alternately wanted to kill him and embrace him."

When Schulberg spoke his mind to Spiegel and Kazan—whose whispering didn't stop—he finally stormed out of the St. Regis suite, slamming the door behind him. Kazan followed, letting Schulberg blow off steam as they stomped from 5th Avenue to 55th Street and back again. Kazan empathized, and they talked about how it was Spiegel's nature to be controlling and so "naturally conspiratorial" in Schulberg's view. For instance, the producer desperately wanted Brando to be closer to him than to Kazan or Schulberg. Schulberg considered Spiegel from the "divide and rule" school. He said, "Instead of being open, he couldn't do that with you. He had to go sneaking around. It was just deep in his psyche to conspire and play one against the other. I don't know where this began, this cat and mouse game." Schulberg complained about all of this to Kazan, who privately referred to Spiegel as "Buddha." The more naturally pugnacious and resilient Kazan assured Schulberg that Spiegel was saying nothing in whispers that couldn't be said aloud. But Kazan's most important rebuttal was irrefutable: "Let's face it, Sam Spiegel has saved our ass." Inevitably, they went back to the St. Regis, but the fight went on for months. In the end, Schulberg conceded, "I'll say this: he had a very, very sharp story mind." And they emerged in late October 1953 with a script on which they were willing to pull the trigger.

Kazan was now ready to form his production crew. As his cinematographer, he chose the Russian American Boris Kaufman. Kaufman, the younger brother of moviemakers Mikhail Kaufman and Dziga Vertov, who photographed and directed, respectively, the stunningly inventive and influential 1929 Russian film *Man with a Movie Camera*. After Boris Kaufman shot several shorts for director Jean Vigo in the late 1920s, he made his mark as cinematographer of two of the same director's most acclaimed films, *Zéro de conduit* and *L'Atalante*. After serving in the French Army, Kaufman had been making ends meet by doing second unit work. That's how Kazan had used Kaufman on *Viva Zapata!*, but the cameraman had yet to handle a feature film assignment. But Kazan, acting on instinct, felt Kaufman was ready for a step up.

They had a shaky start, with Kazan initially sizing up Kaufman as "awfully soft for the job ahead of us and for the place where the job was to be done." In fact, Kazan would begin filming while harboring grave doubts about what he called his "haphazardly gathered" film crew, one of the smallest with whom he had ever worked. Also hired as a technical advisor and location scout was Arthur "Brownie" Brown, who had been so helpful to Schulberg and Kazan in researching the waterfront subculture.

With only three days left before the start of production, Kazan excitedly presented the script to his dramatist wife, Molly Day Thacher, herself a highly influential theatrical light. Having read thousands of plays and advised many young soon-to-be-famous playwrights in her work at the Theater Union, the Group Theater, and the Theater Guild, she read *On the Waterfront* and promptly advised her husband, "The script isn't ready to go," urging him to delay the filming. He reminded her that it was far too late. Not easily deterred, Thacher secretly called Spiegel, insisting that the screenplay still needed major work. For once, Spiegel wouldn't budge. Molly accused him of talking himself and Kazan into believing they had a potential masterwork on their hands. When Spiegel told Kazan and Schulberg about Thacher's phone call, Schulberg was furious. After all, virtually all of Hollywood had rejected, critiqued, and pretty much given the project three days to get out of town. Kazan, Schulberg, and Spiegel had had enough. With or without his estimable wife's stamp of approval, Kazan was moving forward with his movie and with, if possible, an even greater level of righteous rage and resentment than usual.

As for Brando, privately, the actor arrived on set almost lost in a world of trouble and pain. Looming over him was his next assignment immediately after *Waterfront*, *The Egyptian*, a 20th Century Fox Cinemascope costume epic he desperately wanted to get out of. But Darryl Zanuck was forcing on him the dreaded assignment under the terms of a multiple-film contract Brando now deeply regretted having signed. Sam Spiegel scheduled the *Waterfront* filming to begin in the middle of November 1953 primarily on Hoboken, New Jersey's docks, rooftops, streets, and alleyways and in actual tenements, a church, and a dive bar. Although the producer set the stop date for early January 1954, he expected no more than a 30-day shoot. Having whittled down the film's budget to $800,000, with Brando receiving $100,000 and Kazan also drawing $100,000 plus 25 percent of the box-office earnings, Spiegel would time and again make it abundantly clear that if Kazan ran over schedule, he would not hesitate to shut production down and replace him as director. Spiegel set the stage for conflict. And got it.

Elia Kazan wrote himself the following directives on the first page of his *On the Waterfront* shooting script. The first, in red ink:

"PHOTOGRAPH the inner experience OF TERRY." Beneath: "Don't be objective! This is *not* a documentary." No, it was not a documentary. But shooting *On the Waterfront* proved to be a challenging, often unpleasant, contentious experience that was closer to the filming of, say, *Fitzcarraldo* or *Nanook of the North* than a conventional Hollywood entertainment. For some, the set was a battleground. A crucible. A dark comedy of bitterness, feuds, threats, physical violence, betrayals, jealousy, regret, recriminations, and occasionally, grace and camaraderie. In fact, what happened during its 35 days of shooting is in many ways a movie all its own.

November 17, 1953, marked day one of principal photography. Kazan and Kaufman arrived predawn and found trouble already brewing. The scheduled location for that morning's shooting involved three adjoining Hoboken tenement rooftops. Sam Spiegel's production manager had only gotten permission to shoot on the roof of 105 Hudson Street (today, 5 Marine View Plaza) and another two buildings away. The first thing Kazan and Kaufman heard from assistant director Charles H. Maguire (with whom Kazan would later reteam on five more films) was that the owner of the center tenement asked for money. Spiegel stubbornly and typically refused to pay. So shooting any action requiring actors and crew to move from one roof to another required everyone to descend five flights, then up five more flights to the new location. Worse, the heavy cameras, sound equipment, and other technical equipment also had to be lugged up and down all those flights of stairs. Meanwhile, Spiegel was busy striking poses on the roof for a series of press photos with John J. Grogan, who was not only the local mayor but also the vice president of the International Longshoremen's Association. Grogan was out to show the world that unlike the morally compromised characters depicted in the movie, he and his unions were strictly on the up and up. Grinning beside him for the press photographers was the local chief of police. Beside the policeman stood municipal employee

Tony D'Amato, whom Grogan appointed as the liaison between the city and the film company. One of D'Amato's main assignments was to ensure that as many Hoboken residents as possible would make their movie debuts. Spiegel's inserting himself in the photo session was strictly a power move. Schulberg said, "Sam was very aware that being on the set was Gadg's call and he didn't like that."

Meanwhile, Kazan seethed. His keyed-up cast and crew were waiting. Precious time was being frittered away. Once the photographers finally decamped, the assistant director informed Kazan that everyone was ready to get to work. Kazan said, "Not until you clear the roof." First, Maguire escorted away the mayor and police chief. When he returned and announced, "Okay, we're ready," Kazan looked at him pointedly and said, "I told you to clear the roof." Only Sam Spiegel remained behind, puffing a cigar and stalling so he could supervise Kazan and company in action. Directly across the roof, Kazan stared, standing his ground. It was a gun-slinger stand-off worthy of a classic Western. Maguire saw that Kazan would not back down. So the assistant director had to walk over to Spiegel and inform him that Kazan would not make a shot until he was gone. The mogul departed. Wrote Kazan decades later, "That's how I felt about his chiseling and his character that first day and things didn't improve much during the shooting of the film because he chiseled on every cost and took it out of our hides and legs and patience." Things would only worsen as production continued.

For these early rooftop scenes—in fact, for the overall look of the film—Kazan and cinematographer Boris Kaufman wanted to underscore the contrast between gritty Hoboken and the glittering Manhattan skyline in the far distance. But as the old Hollywood axiom goes, *While we plan, the movie gods laugh.* The Hoboken weather delivered something altogether different than what the moviemakers envisioned or as Kazan described it, "the opposite of a picture postcard," that is, gray, foggy, and so brutally cold that the cast had to be given parkas to get them from their lodgings on the southwest corner of Third Avenue and Hudson Street, a hotel named (inaptly) the Grand Hotel. Once they got to the rooftops, the cameras and sound equipment shared space with big metal barrels shooting up flames of burning wood. Kazan raged to Kaufman and anyone within earshot, "Here we are, with the coldest and the grayest and the shortest days coming up, upon a damned roof facing toward a skyline I'd counted on to be a dramatic contrast to the degradation we'd show on the waterfront—and you could hardly see the dammed skyline. There was this mist and smoke from the factory chimneys. When the actors spoke, steam came from their mouths." Kaufman persuaded Kazan to see the weather as a boon, not a curse. He also drew the director's attention to the shapes and textures around them, the jagged edges, fences, sharp railings, and cages everywhere. These elements gave the visuals a trapped, hellish quality. The inner life of Terry, indeed. "All of these conditions created the correct mood for the film, and I wasn't smart enough to realize it immediately," said Kazan. Finally, when the two filmmakers wanted to underscore the harsh realities of the environment, Kaufman learned to simply turn the cameras east.

Brando and Eva Marie Saint's first day of shooting together had them working on those rooftops. They began with the scene of Edie Doyle coming to visit Terry Malloy to give him her dead brother's jacket, and he tenderly shows her his beloved pigeons. Brando laughingly said to Kazan, "You know, it's so fuckin' cold out here that at least there's no way you can overact!" Everyone was bundled up in parkas, removed only moments before filming. Saint arrived, and Kazan realized how out of her element she would be, both as a complete novice to filmmaking and as one of only a few women in the entire production. He told her to imagine that Terry's pigeon coops might just as well be filled with a bear, a gorilla, or a lion. Saint describes her first moments of shooting with a powerful sense of immediacy:

I didn't know Marlon then and I saw him standing over there. My dear, beautiful Kazan watched me and then whispered what he had said during my audition with Marlon: "Eva Marie, in this scene you are really terrified. You don't know anything about men. You've never had an experience with a young man before." He's telling me all this and I'm thinking, "You don't have to say a word. I am already so nervous." In those first days, making my first movie, all these people are watching me. And I kept worrying whether I was going to be any good in it. But Kazan was so good to work for and work with and Marlon was so, so dear. Right away, it was clear that he was one of the finest actors we've ever had. I remember in the beginning, I talked too much to the crew and the other actors on that set. Gadg took me aside and told me to stop doing that. He told me, "Eva Marie, I want you to think of yourself as an hourglass. When you get up in the morning, you've only got so much energy, and that's the sand going through at that rate so that you do not dissipate your energy. If I have a close-up of you, I can't put a card on screening saying, 'Sorry, Eva Marie was just exhausted when she did this close-up.' He wanted me to save my energy and concentrate on the scene. Well, I listened. I never did it again. From then on, on the set, you never saw me talking on the set. You never saw me going out for lunch. I stay focused. I can't really work any other way. Another thing that changed? I wore a coat and a dress in the movie, and both were navy blue. That was such a long time to wear the same clothing and color. I never wore anything navy blue again.

As she began to gain her footing, Saint showed her sense of humor and spirit. When the camera would not reveal it, she wore red tights under her navy-blue skirts. When the spirit moved her, between takes, she'd break out in a jaunty cancan right on the docks, showing those tights. She always won applause.

Schulberg was fascinated by something he observed about Saint while on the set. After she once completed a scene with Brando, Saint got approached by a crew member asking her a question. She didn't hear him. Such was her almost trancelike concentration. Said Schulberg, "That moment really struck me because she was so focused. It was like someone startled her out of a dream. It was one of the qualities that made her so right for the role." Regarding Saint, Schulberg elaborated to a magazine reporter, "You know, there hasn't been anybody like this girl since Vilma Bánky," referring to the Hungarian American who became a major box-office star in the 1920s for producer Samuel Goldwyn and was cast opposite major stars, including Rudolph Valentino and Ronald Colman. She was hailed by *The New York Times* as "a young person of rare beauty . . . exquisite." Critics would later describe Eva Marie Saint similarly.

The third key player in these rooftop scenes was the 14-year-old Thomas Hanley, a non-actor who got cast as one of Terry Malloy's few friends, a fellow loner and pigeon fancier aching with hero worship. At the time of the filming *On the Waterfront*, Hanley and his mother and brother were living near poverty when their 105 Hudson Street apartment building was chosen as the location for the rooftop scenes. He watched the crew building pigeon coops and got by the movie's technical advisor and union reformer Arthur "Brownie" Brown, who had worked with Hanley's dockworker father, Raymond Hanley. When Hanley was four months old, his father, who had spoken out about corruption on the docks, vanished. He was widely believed to have been murdered by the Westies, an Irish gang, on the orders of the West Side pier rats he opposed. Brown got the photogenic Thomas Hanley hired to feed the caged pigeons being used in the film. Some believe that Hanley's hiring was almost a defensive measure. His volatile reputation was widespread enough to raise suspicion, unfairly or not, that he might torch the pigeon coops some night. In any case, Brown soon brought Hanley to the attention of Kazan and Schulberg and arranged for a meeting with them for a role in the film. Hanley said of his audition at the Actors Studio, "They were looking for someone with a temper. Kazan started teasing me about my father, calling him a rat. You know, like, 'Maybe he got killed because he was a squealer.' I became enraged. I went out of my bird and started throwing chairs and punches. After it, they told me, 'That's just what we wanted.' I got the part."

For years, Hanley resented the director's deliberately exploiting his personal tragedy, Method style, both during the screen test and while shooting his scenes with Brando. Recalling filming the memorable "A pigeon for a pigeon" moment when his character reacts to Terry's informing him about dockside corruption by tossing one of his dead pigeons at his feet, Hanley said:

> When [Kazan] wanted to do that scene, he asked me if I thought I could cry or I could show that emotion. I said I really didn't think I could do it. And every time, he would say, "Well, I really think you can." He would talk you through things. He talked to my mother and said, "We want to antagonize him a bit to get him into that mode." She said, "Well, you'll have to ask him." I said, "Let's go for it." [Kazan] brought in this cop that used to live next door. I hated him and he hated me. We were like oil and gasoline. They put us together in the rooftop stairwell. Well, it didn't take long for us to get into a scuffle. Me and him got into a big fistfight. When I was sufficiently enraged—sometimes that's the only time I could cry—they threw me out to do the scene. I did "A pigeon for a pigeon!" a few times, over and over. Everybody said it was great. But I didn't feel that it was so great. I just wasn't tough enough and my character should have been a lot tougher.

Early in the process of filming, Hanley said he needed to over-come his being "in awe of people who I had seen in the movies." But Brando put him at ease for being "a great guy, a lot of fun, just like a regular guy from the streets who took the PATH [Port Authority Trans-Hudson] train instead of a limousine to the set and always came in his costume. He was so nice to me and to my mother." Then there was actor Karl Malden, about whom Hanley said, "He was a real sweetheart of a guy. He would tutor me in what I should watch out for in people." The $500 Hanley made for his two weeks of work on the film paid more than a year's rent on his family's tenement apartment, put something more nourishing on their table than their usual fare of onion soup, and bought them some clothes. Marlon Brando helped land Hanley a talent manager, but aside from an unpaid walk-on for *The Red Skelton Show*, no serious professional opportunities materialized. Hanley found the movie's aftermath unsettling. He said, "I had a lot of girls chasing me, and I didn't know how to handle it." And when he had to quit school and go to work on the docks at age 16, his coworkers constantly taunted and ridiculed him as "the movie star" who blew his big chance at stardom. In the end, he became a longshoreman and a union rep. He retired in 2009.

Hanley, like the entire cast and crew of the movie, recalled the punishing cold. "I lived in Hoboken but I never felt cold and wind like that before, even with the parkas they passed out to everyone every day." As Elia Kazan put it, "The cold was our hardship." But the director had learned on previous films that a director who stands shoulder to shoulder with his crew boosts morale. Meanwhile, Kazan's assistant director, Charles H. Maguire, held in his hand a 10-foot-long piece of string attached to Boris Kaufman's camera and another 10-foot-long string attached to Kazan. As the director put it, "I never had to look for Charlie or he for me. And we never came in out of the weather." Kazan made sure that the actors were only called to the set just before they were needed for a rehearsal or a take. Although Kazan reckoned that his cast suffered most from the weather, he came to believe that the suffering was worth it. He said, "The bite of the wind and the temperature did a great thing for the actors' faces: it made them look like people, not actors."

Despite the hardships the weather imposed, it's a bit of a miracle that no one got sick. Still, Brando complained about the cold, even to reporters who came to the set. More than once, conditions got so brutal that Kazan had to go to Brando's hotel room and virtually drag him to the set. But the director lauded his star's professionalism and gifts, calling him "great, prompt, loaded with talent, full of surprises that improved scenes, a marvelous artist." Assistant director Maguire would go on to work on major films starring Robert Mitchum, Paul Newman, Kirk Douglas, Warren Beatty, and Harrison Ford called Brando the single most professional actor he'd met in his career.

Kazan proved himself adept at dealing with a range of cast members, from his brilliant and turbulent star and his brand-new leading lady to the young, explosive adolescent newcomer. He observed of his actors:

> You have to be able to talk their language. You have to really be able to help them. You have to not be impatient with them. You have to wait them out. You have to have a sense of what's developing in them. You have to have a sense of their process to know when they're getting closer to it or when they need a joke. You have to treat them like kids. You have to be both firm, strong and at the same time, gentle and understanding. You have to coddle them. It's a kind of feminine seduction. They want to be bundled. They want to be hugged and loved. It's sort of nice with a girl. Perhaps a woman should be narcissistic or have allure. But sometimes it's embarrassing in a man to see him playing up to an audience.

As for Brando, "He is exactly the thing I like in actors. There's a hell of a lot of turmoil there. There's ambivalence there . . . an ambivalence between a soft yearning, girlish side to him and a dissatisfaction that can be dangerous."

Meanwhile, Sam Spiegel worked himself into a state about Karl Malden's big speech to the dockworkers. He not only thought Schulberg's speech for Father Barry was preachy and sanctimonious, but he also fretted that if Malden made a meal of the monologue, it might stop the movie cold. He wasn't entirely wrong. Nor was he entirely alone. "I knew that this speech—now transported from the docks to the hold of a ship—could be one of the centerpieces of the movie," Malden said, adding: "But being a worrier, it scared me, too." Kazan set the filming for half the day on a Monday. The Sunday evening just before, Kazan had Malden, his wife Mona, and Brando to dinner at his home; he asked Malden to arrive forty-five minutes early. When the Maldens arrived, Kazan showed the actor into his private study and said, "You've got that big speech tomorrow. I want to hear you do it." Caught off guard, Malden performed the scene twice at Kazan's request—at a rapid clip, with only a few brief pauses to underscore a point or two. "I just want to get the sense of your pace," Kazan explained. What he did not explain was that Spiegel wanted the speech—which timed out at nearly four minutes—cut by at least half. "I'm awfully glad I wasn't aware that I was fighting for my big scene that night in Kazan's study." Not only did Kazan assure Spiegel that he would visually enliven the scene by intercutting reaction shots of extras, but he also had more visceral elements in mind, which he would not disclose.

On shooting day, Kazan told the longshoremen to hurl things at Malden when his speech got especially heated. He tasked the prop master with fabricating a rubber beer can as quickly as possible. But as they made the shot and assistant director Charles Maguire lobbed the rubber beer can, it bounced. Recalls Malden, "I was standing there thinking, 'Uh-oh,'" but he remained quiet. They tried another take, this time with a real beer can, only empty. It floated. Kazan ordered the propman to fill the can halfway with water. Maguire refused to throw it at the well-liked Malden. Nor would anyone else volunteer. "Give me that thing," growled Kazan, grabbing the can from Maguire and climbing up a ladder positioned behind Boris Kaufman's camera, where he had a straight shot at Malden. "You better throw it right," said Malden. Kazan's aim was deadly. He sliced his actor's forehead wide open. Said Malden, "But what was a little blood to a waterfront priest who smoked and drank? I consider it one of my proudest battle scars."

In his obsession with layering into the film as much authenticity as possible, Kazan not only handpicked many locals to populate group and crowd scenes but also selected as many as possible to perform small bits of action and dialogue. He explained, "They lived in Hoboken and suffered the cold and every bit of the difficulty of that life showed in their faces and even the way some walked and held their bodies. I couldn't have gotten that any other way." And so when a longshoreman in the movie's first dockside shape-up scene asks, "Who do you have to see to get a day's pay around here?," it is real-life Hoboken longshoreman Marty Russo who told Kazan and the press that the line came so easily to him because it expressed the kind of anger and frustration he felt every day on the job. Russo later sparks a brawl during the wedding reception. The director handpicked young longshoreman Mike Rubino to play the bridegroom who counsels his new wife at the wedding reception, "You gotta stop smoking so much." Although Kazan had costumer Anna Hill Johnstone doing the first of her six of their movies together and Flo Transfield doing her first of four Kazan movies, the work jacket of murdered dockworker Joey Doyle that is passed to Terry Malloy was lent to the production by actual Hoboken stevedore John Sanducci. When Kazan wasn't getting from Brando the kind of staggering walk he wanted after Terry takes a beating from Johnny Friendly (played by Lee J. Cobb), he turned to longshoreman and ex-fighter James Francis, who had broken away from the gang and demonstrated a rubber-legged walk before collapsing to the ground. The crowd applauded, and Francis took a comic bow. Kazan ordered Brando to ape Francis's movements for retake. They reshot the scene, but Brando was no match for Francis. Kazan considered replacing insert shots of Brando's stumbling legs with those of Francis and also of Hoboken resident and dockworker Anthony DePalma, another face in the crowd. But according to the longtime longshoreman's son Anthony DePalma Jr., today a well-known author and 22-year *New York Times* foreign correspondent, his father—known on the water-front as "Tony-All-The-Time"—*refused* to compromise his reputation for reliability by wasting any extra time indulging in a brief brush with Hollywood fame. When Kazan needed policemen for the movie, he chose such officers of the Hoboken Police Department as Sgt. Pete King. In the courtroom scene, he holds back Lee J. Cobb as Johnny Friendly; later in the film, King tells Terry Malloy, who seethes over being tailed by two police officers, that he "ought to be glad we're following you." Kazan hired E. Rue School gym teacher Frank Marnell to play the man seen switching off the TV during Johnny Friendly's testimony. Marnell gets seen again at the movie's conclusion, this time in support of Terry, as he says to the longshore-men the movie's last line of dialogue, "All right, let's get back to work."

Although Kazan had always wanted Schulberg on the set, the writer only occasionally ventured from Bucks County to Hoboken. As Kazan reasoned, "Why should I make him suffer the weather with the rest of us?" Kazan adhered so closely to the screenplay, there was little point anyway. If Kazan wanted to alter or drop dialogue, he was scrupulous about calling Schulberg to ask permission. On the occasions Schulberg did venture back into Hoboken, Kazan and others remember him mostly heading for a local bar with Brownie or one or another longshoreman. Kazan also had to be able to talk the screenwriter's language. He had promised not to change Schulberg's text, after all, but the locations that became the production's working sets—what Schulberg described as "a frigid Hoboken rooftop, or in a squalid cold-water flat, or in the riverfront saloons"—required dialogue changes. The men struck a deal. The changes would only be made by Schulberg, who was either on the set daily or available on call to make on-the-spot changes. "Oh sure, lines overlapped, good, fresh words were thrown in spontaneously, but scene by scene Gadg stuck to the script, inventing and improving with staging that surprised and delighted me."

Two brooding presences loomed over the filming. First were the organized crime members, so watchful and omnipresent that Schulberg complained of receiving verbal threats and Kazan considered it wisest to hire protection for himself. He found it in the person of Joseph Marotta, brother of Police Chief Arthur Marotta, who carried a gun and kept an eagle eye on him. Marotta proved his worth when a group of Hoboken toughs suddenly rushed the director and pinned him against a wall, pointing fingers and bellowing into his face about how he and his movie were besmirching the good name of Hoboken and its residents (as if *that's* what really triggered their rage). Seeing Kazan surrounded, Marotta lunged at the aggressors, and they scattered. Kazan and Budd Schulberg spoke of receiving many threatening phone calls. Kazan also kept on retainer his posse comprising old-time prizefighters he had hired to play Johnny Friendly's goons—Lee Oma, Tony "Two Ton" Galento, Tami Mauriello, and Abe Simon. Throughout the shoot, Kazan's affection for these men became abundantly clear. "He loved them," said a member of Kazan's stock company set crew. "They were truly colorful guys and, in the movie, they were most like guys you'd see in 30s and 40s gangster movies, Kazan's hulking, scary-funny *opera buffa* characters. He treated them like royalty." There was even more to it, said a Kazan intimate who echoed sentiments voiced by Budd Schulberg and Marlon Brando: "Those tough guys? This was Elia. He liked these guys and felt like he was one of them. You know, a guy off the streets, a scrapper, someone who came up hard. And they responded to him, too."

The second noxious presence on the set was Sam Spiegel. Schulberg exulted in pulling off a passive-aggressive move worthy of Spiegel. In the film, the character played by actor Pat Henning named "Kayo Duggan" (whom Schulberg based on Arthur "Brownie" Brown) gets crushed in a staged "accident." "Father Pete Barry" descends to deliver extreme unction, where he makes his long, impassioned speech about "Christ in the shape-up," the one Spiegel had relentlessly pressed the screenwriter and Kazan to radically trim the speech for fear of grinding the movie to a halt. Given Schulberg's affection and respect for Father Corridan, whose speech was almost verbatim, Spiegel's complaints were a nonstarter. Whenever Spiegel would begin his daily harangue, the screenwriter learned to stay cool and silent and simply walk to a window, throw it open, and stare out, refusing to engage in the pointless discussion. Meanwhile, it was Kazan's job to placate Spiegel by assuring him that sharp editing and cutting to the faces of the old-time fighters who played Friendly's henchmen—the aforementioned Lee Oma, Tony "Two Ton" Galento, Tami Mauriello, and Abe Simon—would take the curse off the talkiness if not the preachy sanctimony. Recalled Schulberg, "After making so much fuss, Mr. S.P. Eagle, the meddlesome bastard, finally gave up on it."

Regularly, Brando reminded Kazan that he had signed on to work with him only because he agreed to shorten his workdays to accommodate his psychiatric appointments in Manhattan. Nevertheless, Brando relied almost as closely on Kazan for guidance on how to play Terry as he had on how to play Stanley in *Streetcar*. Kazan wrote Brando extensive notes on Terry, comparing and contrasting him with Stanley, whom Brando detested as a "Neanderthal man"—one of those "inarticulate, aggressive animals who go through life responding to nothing but their urges and never doubting them."

Well aware of Brando's distaste for Stanley, Kazan called Terry, "a regular, nice guy, a good fellow. He runs with the pack. He is a medium-size hero in the pack and he'd rather give up everything and anything including his dignity and self-worth rather than lose his position in the gang. Terry is lonely, by himself, turned-in, mysterious . . . suspicious of all girls." By comparison, *Streetcar*'s Stanley Kowalski was, wrote Kazan about Brando, "un-self-questioning, un-self-doubting, unaware but Terry was all of those things. Stanley has complete confidence in his cock as the great leveler, the great equalizer. Terry has a similar swagger but his eyes betray him. Marlon, this part is much closer to you, and to myself, too." Kazan viewed loneliness as the key to understanding Terry. Certainly, Brando could empathize with Terry. As for Terry's transformation, his "regaining his dignity or self-esteem," Kazan wrote Brando how he planned "to be photographing the kid's insides as much as the exterior events."

Whether or not Schulberg and Spiegel were on speaking terms became a moment-by-moment-by-moment proposition. On the eve of the first day of shooting, Spiegel reminded Schulberg that he would appreciate the writer's help in keeping Kazan on schedule; he also reminded him of the consequences if Kazan fell behind. But toward Spiegel, there was no love lost. The flamboyant, ostentatious, and blissfully tone-deaf producer bitched and moaned about every penny spent, particularly in the presence of people who were earning near-scale salaries. He continually proffered creative suggestions while warning Kazan not to fall behind schedule. Kazan said, "The crew used to refer to him as 'that Jew bastard.'" Warnings of an all-out mutiny by the crew grew so menacing and constant that if Kazan hadn't interceded several times on Spiegel's behalf, the director was certain that "some violence would have happened." Here is one particular incident that might have been the trigger. Kazan was filming Brando and Saint discovering the body of his murdered brother hanging on a meat hook. It was punishingly cold, and the actors were exhausted and freezing, and the hour was late. Spiegel's limousine pulled up, and he debarked flouting a bespoke camel hair coat, leather gloves, and alligator shoes. The producer watched the filming and began carping to anyone within earshot that Kazan was running over schedule, costing Spiegel because of his fussy perfectionism. The crew grew restive. Hearing Spiegel's insults, Kazan laced into him, threatening to walk out on the spot. The crew and actors backed him up. Spiegel stood down. When they were filming in the 1960s, Kazan told his *Splendor in the Grass* star Warren Beatty that Spiegel's "heart is full of shit. And if you repeat that, I'll deny it." Whenever Kazan spoke publicly in later years about Spiegel, he insisted that *On the Waterfront* would have failed without Spiegel's interventions and inventions.

Spiegel, however, remained Spiegel. On another evening, Kazan and the crew were filming an action sequence involving a crew member driving a truck aimed straight at Marlon Brando and Eva Marie Saint, who were hurtling down the narrow cobblestone alleyway of Court Street, which runs from Newark to Seventh Streets. Things easily could have gone very wrong. Says Saint, "We were to run down an alley with the truck coming straight for us. The door of one building was supposed to be unlocked so that we could dive in. Well, that truck came at us much too fast, and the unlocked door turned out to be locked. Marlon had to smash the glass and hurt his hand doing it. We got inside the doorway but, oh, that truck got very close. It was very dangerous." They got the scene then, suddenly, Spiegel materialized. He and one of his ever-revolving merry-go-rounds of increasingly younger beauties alighted from the limousine dressed to the nines with their breath, Schulberg quipped, redolent of "Chateaubriand from 21." Spiegel came down so loudly and publicly on Kazan that the director started to lunge at Spiegel then stopped himself at the last moment, turned on his heels, and stormed away.

Kazan made a beeline straight for Schulberg and growled, "Budd, I've had it. I warned that son of a bitch if he came on this set once more and broke our concentration, I was gonna quit! I'm not going to let the son of a bitch near the set again." To calm Kazan, Schulberg threw back the director's own words to him: "Gadg, one thing you've got to remember. We were down to our last out. Let's face it, Sam Spiegel saved our ass." Kazan got the joke. He led Spiegel and his companion back into their limo and went back to work.

Considering Marlon Brando's status as a sex symbol, being rampantly sexual and an inveterate seducer, it is not surprising that some working on the production presumed that the potent chemistry between the star and the leading lady might result in a love affair. But in the decades since they worked together, Saint has recalled her then-30-year-old costar only as "adorable and dear." She said:

> I think in those days he was so happy to be acting. He was a prince of princes. To work with him was wonderful. He was so attentive, so talented, so super sensitive that, off camera, I felt a little self-conscious around him. I kept wondering what he was thinking of me—of Eva Marie, that is, not of the actress. Of course, once you start working and you're the character, then he's the character. You're playing those two people. What was a little scary about him, but which worked for me in the movie, was his keen perception of other people. He could look at somebody or talk with them and hone into what that person was all about. He would mention to me his perceptions of people around us. Sometimes I would sit there thinking, "If he knows that about *that* person, he must know more about me than I know about myself." I felt like he could see right through me, that he knew more about me than I knew about myself. It made me a little self-conscious, but, again, I used that in the movie. [Terry] had been out in the world and I had been at home protected, so I used that in playing Edie.

She later said, "Marlon was mysterious. I'd like to be a little more mysterious."

## Glove Story

By now, the scene of Terry and Edie conversing as they walk through a bleak, wintry park—and Edie accidentally dropping her glove—has attained legend. And that may be because, as with most Hollywood legends, it hinges on irresistible absurdities and clichés. In a supposedly hard-hitting, anti-Hollywood movie, the scene is as wonderfully realized a moment of conventional Hollywood-style romance as it comes. After all, from their opening moments together in the movie, Kazan, Schulberg, and Brando sell so forcefully the broken-down, anguished, lonely Terry that the audience is virtually *commanded* to empathize and feel pity for him. Meanwhile, Saint conveys Edie's convent-educated innocence and moral purity with rare, moonstruck guilelessness. By the time of their walk in the park, we're pulling for these two unlikely characters to find a spark of affection in a cold world—so much so that we actually fall into a swoon over a fumbling, tentative romance between a tenement madonna and the misunderstood brute who, after all, helped lead her brother to his death. Talk about punch-drunk love.

Of filming the scene in the park, Saint recalls:

> Kazan would be directing the scene at hand, but if you weren't in that scene, you were always supposed to be rehearsing for the next scene about to come up. So we were always, always rehearsing. When Gadg wasn't filming and was waiting, say, for the lighting men to light a particular scene, he would come watch you wherever you were rehearsing and comment. After that, he'd go back to the scene at hand. So, Marlon and I were working the scene with the glove and it's the first time, as this sheltered,

inexperienced young Catholic woman, I'm really talking to this young person of the opposite sex. That's a difficult scene. Why would a Catholic girl who didn't know about the opposite sex stay there and talk to this guy? So as Marlon and I were rehearsing, I took off my gloves and dropped one by mistake. When I started to pick up my glove, Marlon leaned over and picked it up instead. But he didn't give it back to me. Instead, Marlon, the actor—completely in character—put the glove on his own hand. I mean, it was very sensuous what he did with that glove. It worked for the scene because, that way, this shy, inexperienced girl *had* to stay and talk with him to get back her glove. Gadg was watching us rehearse, and when he saw what we had done, he said, "Exactly the way you two just rehearsed it, that's the way I want it in the film." There have been so many different versions and renditions of the story of that scene and that damn glove. There are those who say that the script was written that way. It wasn't. What I've just said—that is the true story. It shows what an incredible, brilliant actor Marlon was. It shows the genius of Marlon Brando. I'm convinced that, in rehearsal, any other actor would have picked up the glove and handed it to me. We'd have just gone back to rehearsing, that would have been that, and then we'd be up at bat before the camera.

Some weeks later, Brando and Saint set pulses racing when they filmed the scene during which Terry bursts into Edie's apartment after Edie learns that Terry was complicit in the death of her brother. Karl Malden, who observed the filming, believed that Brando drove the scene: "It was all Marlon." Initially, Saint encountered difficulty in playing the scene as Terry turns up the erotic heat, a replay of the improvised scene she and Brando enacted during her audition for Kazan. She said, "The house we were using was actually the house of a newly married Hoboken couple. I felt so badly, they should be starting their life together. But I got over that." Kazan noted that the well-brought-up, modest, and diffident Saint appeared highly uncomfortable filming with Brando wearing only a slip. Karl Malden offered another opinion: "I think [Eva Marie] was a little frightened of him." After all, Brando's innate sensuality and physicality, not to mention his powers of seduction, were already gossip column and magazine story fodder. At just the right moment before attempting a take, Kazan took Saint aside and whispered her husband's name, "Jeffrey." That lit a fire. Although Saint at first resisted, according to Malden, "[Brando] was so good that she gave in and really went with it." The scene's improvisational feel helped the actors create some of the most raw and intimate moments in American cinema up to that time. According to Malden, everyone present felt the heat.

Once Brando and Kazan knew that they had achieved exactly what they needed from the scene, Brando glanced at Saint and with an innocently knowing grin, said, "Well, *that* was something!" Saint has said of filming such moments with Brando, "He was funny. Every take was different, and you really had to listen because depending on the inflection and the intent of the question, you must go along with that and make sense of it. It just kept you on your toes and made it so fresh. [After filming that scene], I was so nervous; I cried a little." The scene, she said, turned out "beautiful." Kazan told Schulberg and others how moved he was by Brando's most tender moments, especially those with Saint. Even decades after the film's release, the director expressed to movie critic and author Richard Schickel, "When he plays those scenes with her, I'm broken up. I break up. That one person should need so much from another person in the way of tenderness and all that. We all do, don't we? The thing about Brando—I mean, who knows where the genius was born, or how it arrives?—but he is a genius. But if he hadn't been so beautiful, he might never have been seen, encouraged, hired. The beauty was the runway on which the genius could walk. These are accidents of God and genes and luck. Take your pick. He was the entire package." Speaking with

Schickel in the mid-1990s, Kazan rhapsodized about Brando's work, "It seems to me however fine the script is and however fine the look of the picture, there's something in that performance that just tears your heart out. I'm not sure that's inherent in the script. The thing about Brando is there is . . . both a toughness, an exterior roughness, and a tremendous desire for gentleness and tenderness. And the best scenes in the movie, from my point of view, are the ones with Eva Saint where he's asking her to understand him, like when they're sitting in the café. He's great in those scenes. Why? Because he's a tough guy revealing a side of himself you don't expect."

Admittedly, Brando could occasionally be a handful. Although he spent hours hanging out with the longshoremen and the amateur actors, Brando, Kazan recalled, would "often come on the set sleepy, tired, exhausted and he sometimes needed me saying something that he didn't like for him to become rejuvenated or alive. In films, you just work differently with every actor. You use any means necessary." Kazan initially noted Brando's having some hesitation in his scenes with Saint. When he took the actor aside and asked what was wrong, said the director, "Marlon said he didn't know how to flirt with Eva's character—as Terry, the character he was playing. He knew how to flirt as Marlon Brando, which was direct, a bit poetic, strong. How could he be simple and sweet and a bit unsure? He said he remembered a gesture both his mother and his sister utilized when they were flirting—a touch to the hair, a leaning in, a softening of the eyes. It's in the film." And it worked beautifully not only onscreen for Terry's courtship of Edie but also offscreen for Saint, who found herself as sympathetic to Brando as a person as she was deeply impressed by Brando's exceptional talent. Kazan and others remembered Brando's solicitousness toward Saint and how he'd remove his plaid jacket and draped it around her shoulders whenever she looked especially cold. Although Brando and Saint attempted to enjoy each other's company when they were not filming, things did not go as easily.

When we'd have lunch and he was Marlon and I was Eva Marie, not Terry and Edie, I was self-conscious. He wasn't part of the Actors Studio but I'd seen him in class though never actually worked with him before. That can happen. I felt the same way about Monty Clift when I did *Raintree County*. When you're working, the catalyst is the material, the scene, what you're creating. Then that stops. I remember one day Monty asked me to have lunch with him. I used to be much shyer than I am now. I still am shy when I'm with a lot of people, like at a party. So at lunch, Monty and I put down our menus and he didn't say anything. I felt panicky. It was one of the few times in my life where I was tongue-tied. I didn't know what to say. I didn't know what to do. So, as I remember, we just ate our lunch. I couldn't wait for us to get through that lunch and go back to the set where we had lines and he had to say something to me. But he was very sweet and very quiet and very reserved. I think there's a part of me that's bashful, still. When I'm with someone like that it's difficult for me to bring them out like a therapist would do or like somebody. . . . I couldn't do it.

Saint might have found a more talkative Brando at one of his favorite hangouts while on location, Serventi's Restaurant (aka Clam Broth House) at 36–42 Newark Street, except for the fact that the famed dockworker's hangout had been strictly men-only since 1900 and only finally opened its doors to women in 1970 under threat of a lawsuit. Even today, though, locals recall Brando for his friendliness while enjoying beers and buckets of steamed clams in the company of the stevedores. He would often arrive alone or in the company of Karl Malden and, less often, Lee J. Cobb. No one has reported whether Brando ever ran into another Serventi's habitué, such as Frank Sinatra, who lived until age 12 at nearby 415 Monroe Street and regularly returned to the old neighborhood to dine in the company of his mother, Dolly.

Most of Brando's *Waterfront* coworkers recall his being amiable and professional on the set, posing few of the alleged problems that made him a gossip column staple. Most of Brando's *Waterfront* coworkers recall his being amiable and professional on the set, posing few of the alleged problems that made him a gossip column staple, even when he didn't warrant it. Case in point: during the movie's production, several newspaper columnists reported that after heated disagreements with Kazan over creative matters, Brando walked off the set. Yet one famous incident that sparked a lifelong feud stemmed from Brando's dislike of a scene that would go on to become the most famous of the entire production.

## Taxi

By now, the betrayal scene between mobbed-up Charley (Rod Steiger) and his deluded younger brother Terry in the back seat of a taxi has been fossilized in the amber of legend. It is a scene as emblematic of *On the Waterfront* as the shower murder in *Psycho*, the "Rosebud" reveal in *Citizen Kane*, or Travis Bickle's "Are you talking to me?" moment with the mirror in *Taxi Driver*. On the day of shooting this scene, which would go on to become one of the most famous in film history, circumstances were less than ideal. Though nearly everyone who read Budd Schulberg's screenplay felt its power and empathized and even wept, Brando dug in his heels and flatly refused to film what he termed "an unplayable scene." "He had a marvelous quality of stubbornness," observed Kazan of Brando.

> On this movie, I would several times go up to Brando and say, "I want you to do so and so" . . . and then there'd be this awesome silence in which he'd look at me as though I were the fool of the world and [then would] say, "You don't really mean that, do you?" And I'd say, "Well, yes I do." He'd say, "Well, that's terrible.

I just can't do that. That seems false." Usually, he was right. But he always had an idea of his own. He'd sort of walk away, scratch his head and go talk to somebody, usually an assistant like this sort of a half hairdresser, half makeup man he had with him, a Spanish boy who [became] an assistant producer to him later. He'd go talk with him, come back and always have something that was good, often better than I did.

Recalls Budd Schulberg, "The very first day's shooting, I was up on the roof of the tenement in Hoboken with Kazan and Brando. Someone happened to bring up the taxicab scene that we would be shooting sometime later. I knew Marlon was already making some trouble about it. I said: 'You know, Marlon, everybody loves that scene except you. Why?' He said, 'Steiger has a gun. If someone is pointing a gun at you, you're not going to make a long speech like that.' And Kazan just said, 'Why don't you just push his gun aside?' That was the end of the argument. Apart from that, Marlon was very amenable." And apart from that simple motivation Kazan gave to Brando, the director said the scene required little else from him: "I didn't do any directing there. The cab scene was written so well and [Brando and Steiger] understood it." But those involved recall the details and the dissension differently. Rod Steiger maintains that it was a grip, not Kazan, who suggested to Brando that he push away the gun. Said Steiger, "Being as talented and bright as he is, [Brando] took that right away. I didn't know he was going to do it. In the first place, when I work I don't like to know what people are going to do. It takes away from the spontaneity. The back seat scene works, number one, because of Marlon's talent. Number two, it's almost a love scene between two brothers. I don't mean sexually but there is such a feeling of *simpatico* between the two, even though one is doing something wrong, he's still your brother. And he looks at me and I'm still his brother. That added a certain compassion and intensity, I think."

The fact that both actors understood the scene didn't help the shooting proceed smoothly, though. For one thing, there was the built-in issue of the filming locale: a tiny studio space no larger than a long, narrow room. "If we put our arms out the [car] window, we would have hit a wall," Steiger said of it. Then, there was the taxi itself. Because Brando, Steiger, and Kazan prided themselves on making a realistic, proudly non-Hollywood production, they fully expected they would be filming in an actual New Jersey cab. But producer Spiegel's penny-pinching struck again. Recalls Steiger, "The taxi was an old, beaten-up prop from an old TV studio." And instead of a rear projection setup—pre-filmed footage of dark urban streets projected onto a screen in the background while Brando, Steiger, and Nehemiah Persoff (as the taxi driver) played the scene live in the foreground—there was *nothing* outside the car windows. When called out, Spiegel claimed that he had simply "forgotten" to pay for the rental of the back projection equipment. After all the corner cutting and pressure Spiegel had put Kazan through, the director didn't buy the flimsy explanation for a second. He bellowed at the producer, "How the hell can I shoot the scene if you can see through the back of the cab and five feet away is the wall of the studio? You were supposed to get back projection!"

The shooting schedule and budget were too tight to do anything but improvise a quick fix. Enter the venetian blinds and some prop men aiming lights at the actors to suggest oncoming traffic. Steiger said, "The venetian blind wasn't there when we got on the set. And the thing that saved us is one of the working men on the crew said, 'Do you know, I came to work in a cab that had a venetian blind?' And Kazan, who's no fool said, 'Get me a bloody venetian blind!' It took several hours to rejigger the scene and ready it for shooting." Installing the venetian blind and having nothing going on outside the cab windows, said Steiger, "forced them to stay in close with the camera. So basically, it depended on the two actors. It also added a tension for the actors." During that time, actor Nehemiah Persoff, who played the cabdriver perched on a wooden box substituting for the nonexistent front seat, sought Kazan's advice on how to play the scene. Kazan advised: "Play it as though Charley killed your mother."

Hours later, once the venetian blinds had been mounted onto the back window, the crew and cast members were good to go. The atmosphere certainly didn't lack for personal and professional tension between Steiger and Brando. Brando refused to let go of his insistence that audiences would never buy the idea that Terry would deliver such an impassioned speech while his brother had a gun pointed at him. Brando even wrote of it in his autobiography, calling the notion "absurd" as written in the screenplay. Kazan huddled with Brando, Steiger, and Schulberg to address the actor's concerns. Kazan proposed that Charley would lower the gun before Terry speaks, and everyone signed off on the change. Shooting the scene, Brando and Steiger improvised dialogue, with Brando peppering his fellow actor with such questions as "How's mom?" and "Do you think the Giants or the Indians will take the World Series this year?" Kazan grew weary of the fun and games and counseled the actors, "Just say the lines." It was a familiar Kazan prescription. Eva Marie Saint similarly recalled Kazan's offering the same corrective instructions when the director thought actor John F. Hamilton was becoming too melodramatic when playing Edie Doyle's father, "Pop."

But Brando didn't strictly adhere to the script, and the scene is the better for it. Consider Schulberg's version of the most often quoted part of Terry's speech. The final revised shooting version of the screenplay reads "I could've been a contender. I could've had class and been somebody. Real class. Instead of a bum, let's face it, which is what I am. It was you, Charley." During filming, Brando did not wait for Steiger to lower the gun. Instead, he pushed it down himself and then said, "I could have had class. I could have been a contender. I could've been somebody, instead of a bum. Which is what I am, let's face it. . . . It was you, Charley." Small, subtle changes, yes, but that made the speech sound more spontaneous, emotional, heartbreaking, and in character. Karl Malden watched the scene being shot and marveled at one of Brando's unscripted contributions when, after Terry pushes down the gun, Brando looked away, drew his hand toward his face, and quietly muttered "Wow" in realization of his brother's betrayal. Said Malden, "This is where his genius comes in. You know exactly what he's thinking . . . he put himself in the situation." And he made Terry's situation and the deterioration of the brothers' relationship immediately relatable and all the more devastating to the audience.

Revealed Steiger:

Nobody knows what really goes on in a scene. We did Brando's close-up and I was off camera. When you're off camera with another actor, you do your nut. You overdo it to help them with reaction. And, in that scene, you might say, off camera, to help the actor: "I gotta tell you something. I hate your guts. Do you understand? I hate you. You're no good. You're stupid. You couldn't act if your life depended on it. How did you get in this film?" Anyway, at the time, Brando was the toast of the town, Broadway and Hollywood. When we filmed the backseat scene, we filmed it the usual way, the master shot of us both, again with a close-up on Brando and then with my close-up. When you get to a scene like that, it's best to let the words take you where it's going. And I got so upset trying to save [Terry's] life that I pulled the gun on him, threatening him so he'll agree and saying, *You've got to go*. Acting is reacting. So we're very dependent on each other. I stayed to deliver my lines from off camera to Brando when he did his close-ups, but when it came time for my close-up, Mr. Brando left, walked away. I never forgot that. It was like a wounding. I couldn't believe that a man that talented would walk out. It's the lowest. I had to do my close-up with the stage manager there reading [Brando's] lines off camera. So, it must have burned [Brando's] rear end because we came out even in that scene.

In 1957, Brando told Truman Capote in a *New Yorker* interview, "That was a seven-take scene and I didn't like the way it was written. Lot of dissension going on there. I was fed up with the whole picture. All the location stuff was in New Jersey and it was the dead of winter—the cold, Christ! And I was having problems at the time. Woman trouble. That scene . . . there were seven takes because Steiger couldn't stop crying. He's one of those actors who loves to cry. We kept doing it over and over. But I can't remember just how it crystallized itself for me." To Brando, the scene's power and lasting impact had "nothing to do with me. The audience does the work. They are doing the acting. Everybody feels like they're a failure. Everybody feels they could have been a contender. Inferiority . . . I've been very close to it all my life."

Kazan reiterated, "I didn't do any directing with it, you can believe it. It's true. I'm not a falsely modest man. They did it. They made the scene, those two men." One of the great ironies of *On the Waterfront*—made by fiercely independent, rebellious spirits who set out to make a defiantly un-Hollywood movie—is that its most famous scene is as old Hollywood as it gets. The opposite of naturalistic in technique, it was filmed on a soundstage, using artificial technical effects and minimal lighting and props but written and performed at the level of tragic grand opera—by two men.

As the production wore on, Kazan conveyed his mood and mental state in a letter written to Tennessee Williams in late December 1953:

> I'm pooped, the picture being physically very tough and no where [*sic*] near over. I have to face not only the elements, the racket guys, the longshoremen and an uncut script but also the consternation, daily reinforced, of a rapidly-becoming-bankrupt Producer. The whole thing is taking almost twice as long as he planned, what with my stubbornness and the five hours of photographable daylight. I'm between feeling sorry for [Spiegel]

and cautioning myself almost hysterically not to feel sorry for him and to stick to making the picture good. The several times I've been motivated by anything but getting [a] halfway decent film, the day's work stank. And so—I'm tired. The actors have been wonderful, however, wonderful. Brando looks older and a little heavier but is better than ever. He has new "manly" qualities of tenderness and dignity and relaxation and humor. I mean relaxed humor, not eccentric humor. He's a most unusually honest artist and has saved me many times from doing things that are phony. I'm very fond of him, really love him, yet there is no way to express it to him. Malden and Lee Cobb are both magnificent, and a new girl, Eva Saint [*sic*], makes a rather foolish part believable (I hope)—let's say playable. Anyway, the actors act like comrades and colleagues and are loyal and endure cold and penny-pinching equally well. I'm very heartened by them. My God they're wonderful. . . . There are a few old school small parts and about five former boxing "Greats" who lend just a touch of fantasy to the whole proceedings. The Racket Mob send their people to observe from the fringes and they listen and smile a little foolishly at the erratically flung off bits of dialogue. It's weird. Well I'll be another few weeks, and then I'll rest.

When Kazan wrapped the movie in 35 days on January 25, 1954, Spiegel insisted that he should have been able to do it faster. Said Kazan, "I never turned against Sam, no matter what he did because he made the picture better. Zanuck could never have done that." Yet more often than he ever intended, Kazan reportedly had the crews working 12 hours overtime. It was a brutal shoot. Still, Eva Marie Saint said on completing filming, "I loved every minute, in fact, next to my marriage, it's been the highlight of my life. When we were finished, I wept." She told the press that the experience had "spoiled" her because she had "the best of everything: the best in stories, direction, players to work with. I hated to see it end." Kazan told her—and the world—that he thought her "a wonderful young actress" with a bright future and hoped to work with her again. But that never happened.

Days after completing his final scene in *Waterfront*, Brando celebrated by hosting a party in suite 801, his eighth-floor 57th Street apartment above Carnegie Hall. Many of his immediate neighbors crammed into the apartment, mingling with close friends and family, including his sister Jocelyn Brando, actress Maureen Stapleton, singer–comedian Kaye Ballard, and Brando's friend since childhood, Wally Cox, the droll, deadpan star of the hit TV comedy series about an erudite high school teacher *Mister Peepers*. Cox spent much of the night sitting on the arm of Brando's chair. Also present was one of Brando's current girlfriends, Josanne Mariani-Berenger. Brando had met the fisherman's daughter while finding a welcome respite from public scrutiny in Bandol, France, near Toulon. He told friends and the press that one of the reasons he and Mariani-Berenger got on so well was that she cared nothing about show business or his white-hot fame at the time. He had announced their engagement but would soon break off the relationship. Also in his life at the time, though absent from the party, was the actress Movita (Castaneda), who had often been cast as sloe-eyed exotics in such 1930s entertainments as *Top Hat*, *The Hurricane*, and the Clark Gable–Charles Laughton version of *Mutiny on the Bounty*. They would marry in 1960. Several *Waterfront* cast and crew members—including Karl Malden—also attended Brando's personal wrap party. Elia Kazan, however, was not invited. Working together again had done little to mend their fractured relationship.

And with the party over, Brando, declaring his time filming *Waterfront* "the most miserable I've ever been in my life," was about to be threatened by Darryl Zanuck and 20th Century Fox with a highly publicized $2 million lawsuit unless he reported to work on *The Egyptian*, an overblown project for which he foresaw doom. He begged Dr. Mittelman to send the studio's lawyers psychiatric reports of his being "very sick and confused" and unfit to work for 10 weeks. To avoid the detectives Zanuck sent to find him, Brando reportedly "dressed like a United Nations Diplomat" in public but mostly became a fugitive in his and others' apartments. He dodged phone calls, fearing his agent or Zanuck would be on the line. He surrendered to an internal anguish, self-doubt, and loathing that had been a long time coming. In March, his mother died unexpectedly. It was his coup de grâce. But it persuaded Zanuck to release him from *The Egyptian*; as recompense, the mogul forced him instead to play Napoleon in the frustratingly subdued historical slog, *Désirée*.

# Six

# Postproduction

## *Enter the Maestro*

**B**y the late spring, Kazan and editor Gene Milford were ready with a rough cut. Milford, a former stuntman, had been cutting pictures since 1926 and joined Columbia in 1929, editing such movies as Frank Capra's *Lost Horizon*, for which he won an Oscar. Working with Kazan on *Waterfront*, Milford so quickly learned how to best showcase the rapidly changing cadences of American acting styles that he completed the editing in a matter of weeks. When Sam Spiegel emerged from the rough-cut screening, he asked Kazan point blank if he thought the public would pay to see the movie. To Kazan, it was like Darryl Zanuck saying all over again *Who's going to give a shit about a bunch of sweaty longshoremen?* But maybe Spiegel's question wasn't as crass or crazy as it sounded. In 1954, when American moviegoers seemed more attuned to big, shiny entertainments, such as *Demetrius and the Gladiators, Rear Window, 20,000 Leagues Under the Sea* and, yes, (oh the irony) *The Egyptian, On the Waterfront* was an outlier. Spiegel wanted to salvage his reputation and climb out of the deep financial hole he had dug for himself. He was, said Kazan, "anxious to get another prominent name on the advertising copy." The more cynical Budd Schulberg thought Spiegel's discomfort ran deeper, that he lost whatever little faith he had in *On the Waterfront* to begin with.

Thirty-five-year-old Leonard Bernstein was pretty much anyone's idea of a major catch, an eminently prominent name for the advertising copy. Widely renowned as the conductor of the New York Philharmonic, a celebrated composer of Broadway musicals (*Wonderful Town* and *On the Town*), a ballet (*Fancy Free*, which birthed *On the Town*), and a symphonic concert piece for orchestra and piano (*The Age of Anxiety*), there wasn't a starrier name in American classical music than Bernstein's. Add to these achievements his flair for showmanship in and out of the spotlight, his dashing good looks, his charisma and vitality, and the gilt-edged international social circles in which he traveled. In other words, Bernstein exuded the level of cachet Spiegel loved flaunting on a movie poster, as well as putting on display at his famously sybaritic dinner parties.

An ardent moviegoer, Bernstein had Hollywood come knocking before on his door. In April 1943, movie studio titan Jack Warner proffered him a substantial five-year contract to compose musical scores for Warner Bros.; the offer came with the tempting promise of a weekly paycheck the profligate Bernstein could have used at the time. Bernstein's friend and collaborator, Broadway and film composer Adolph Green, wrote warning Bernstein against allowing himself to be seduced by the movie business. That said, Green also promised his work would surely be embraced by Warner's session musicians, especially "after all the [Max] Steiner–[Erich] Korngold crap they've been playing." For years, another close colleague, the esteemed and influential composer Aaron Copland, shared with Bernstein his highs and lows while creating scores for such movies as *The Red Pony* and *The Heiress*. Copland warned in a letter that Hollywood was "not creative country . . . (except when you're paid)." Despite the caveats, Bernstein accepted the contract. But in a May 29 letter to fellow composer-conductor Serge Koussevitzky, he was already describing his work for Warner Bros. as "dull beyond belief" and a series of "horrible chores." Small wonder that Bernstein and

the studio drifted apart by summer's end. Smaller wonder that Warner Bros. never credited Bernstein with making a musical contribution to any of their films.

The year 1945 brought him a very different kind of interest
from Hollywood. This time, the invitation came from Paramount
Pictures–based Hal B. Wallis, producer of *Little Caesar*, *Casablanca*,
and *The Maltese Falcon*. Fond of making entertaining but highly fan-
ciful "biographical" movies, Wallis wanted to launch a musical film
based on the relationship between Pyotor Ilyich Tchaikovsky and his
great patroness, Baroness Nadezhda von Meck, who forbade them
from ever meeting. To play Madame von Meck, Wallis courted the
interest of no less than Greta Garbo, who, at 35, had turned her back
on Hollywood five years earlier. Irving Rapper (*Now, Voyager* and *The
Corn Is Green*) was set to direct the Tchaikovsky–von Meck film from
an Ayn Rand screenplay. In late May 1945, Bernstein attended—as the
invited guest of Wallis and Rapper—the New York premiere of their
shamelessly fictional film biography of Gershwin, *Rhapsody in Blue*.

Wallis initially discussed with Bernstein the possibility of his
being hired as musical advisor on the Tchaikovsky film. But after
meeting with him, the self-described "star maker" had more ambitious ideas. Having helped launch and promote the film careers of
Humphrey Bogart, Bette Davis, Errol Flynn, and Burt Lancaster, and
in the 1950s, Shirley MacLaine, Elvis Presley, Dean Martin, and Jerry
Lewis, among others, Wallis was on the hunt for a new "discovery"
to portray the tortured, sexually conflicted Tchaikovsky. He thought
he might have found his man in the 27-year-old Bernstein. A lifelong Tchaikovsky admirer, Bernstein once said conducting a truly
inspired performance of Tchaikovsky's work required him to *become*
Tchaikovsky. How's that for hinting to Hollywood that you're ready
for your close-up?

Meanwhile, Rapper shifted into overdrive. He and Bernstein
rendezvoused at the swank Hotel Reforma in Mexico City, and

the ardent director arranged what his guest called in a letter to his personal assistant "a series of events that would knock your eyes out." They included two dinner parties, a concert conducted by the renowned Carlos Chávez, a day at the races, a party, a bullfight, and more, including, as Bernstein wrote, "drinking, sex, lassitude, futility and *expatrié snobisme.*" In between all this, he accepted Rapper's invitation to a dinner party at his home that Bernstein thought was a prelude to discussing a possible screen version of the ballet *Fancy Free.* Instead, it was a party to announce a decision by Wallis and Rapper to screen-test Bernstein for the leading role in their proposed Tchaikovsky biopic.

On the evening of June 24, 1945, Rapper feted his potential movie star in his Hollywood home. Even a partial guest list impresses: Somerset Maugham, Cary Grant, Judy Garland, George Cukor, Ethel Barrymore, Joan Fontaine, Dana Andrews, Van Johnson, and Bette Davis. Rapper, who had directed Davis in five movies, had learned that she was Bernstein's favorite star. The director made certain to give the two maximum chances to interact throughout the evening. Although Bernstein loathed being forced to "sing" for his supper, he acceded to Davis's request for him to play a Tchaikovsky piece on the piano. He invited her to sit beside him on the piano bench. Things got so chummy that Rapper later agreed to pass along to Bernstein a touching letter in which Davis conveyed how the musician's "mighty talents" had lifted her at a time when she had "hit a new low." With Bernstein's return to New York, the two began exchanging letters and telegrams.

There is no reason to believe that Davis was being insincere in those letters. There may be some reason to suspect that Davis was waiting in the wings hoping to be cast as Madame von Meck in Rapper's film if the mercurial Garbo pulled out. In a missive she signed as "B. Von Meck," she playfully asks Bernstein if he'd mind her becoming "a 1945 version of Madame von Meck." Meanwhile, Rapper oversaw the details of Bernstein's screen test scheduled to be shot in New York, consisting of several monologues from Ayn Rand's screenplay and Bernstein's playing Tchaikovsky's "The Grand Piano Sonata in G major, Op. 37." Shirley Bernstein, who herself would go on to become a film and TV producer, acted as her older brother's dialogue coach. She recalled their "roaring helplessly over the silliness of the writing" and the screenplay's being "terribly written." As for Bernstein's attempts at acting? "Equally terrible," his sister declared. "He didn't have the talent and he was far too quick to see the ridiculous side of himself." Minus Garbo and a good screenplay, Wallis and Rapper's Tchaikovsky project vaporized. Probably mercifully.

The year 1949 offered another brush with Hollywood, also for better or worse. Although *On the Town* made Bernstein and his longtime friends and colleagues Betty Comden and Adolph Green the proverbial toasts of Broadway in 1944, Bernstein was powerless to stop *An American in Paris* and *Singin' in the Rain* producer Arthur Freed and MGM from having Roger Edens, Comden, and Green replace all but four of Bernstein's original songs. Meanwhile, Bernstein continued to turn down other offers to score films; he would go on to explain later, "on the grounds that it is a musically unsatisfactory experience for a composer to write a score whose chief merit ought to be its unobtrusiveness." To Sam Spiegel, a font of Hollywood insider gossip and inveterate star-fucker, all of this made Bernstein irresistible.

In early 1954, Spiegel began his full-on courtship of Bernstein for *On the Waterfront*. Bernstein begged off. As usual, his conducting services and recording schedule kept him in constant demand. Also, as usual, he was firing off ideas for new projects, such as the possibility of a new biblically themed opera for the CBS television series *Omnibus*, based on the friendship of David and King Saul, which was dramatized in J. M. Barrie's play *The Boy David*. Also looming large was his and Lillian Hellman's decision to abandon their Eva Perón opera to instead reignite the work they'd begun in 1953 on an opera based on Voltaire's brilliantly satirical novella, *Candide*. The HUAC hearings that led to Hellman's 1948 blacklisting and the FBI's obsession with Bernstein's leftist politics compelled both collaborators to use *Candide* to comment on the excesses and hysteria of the McCarthy era. And so, when Spiegel offered Bernstein *On the Waterfront*—a film directed and written by and celebrating an informer— no wonder he balked. In the end, Spiegel's begging and wheedling eventually piqued his curiosity enough to get him to agree to attend a private screening of the rough cut.

Bernstein recalled experiencing the film, particularly Brando's performance, with "a surge of excitement" that led to his "being swept by enthusiasm into accepting the commission to write the score." He said he heard music as he watched the movie, and even more, "the atmosphere of talent that this film gave off was exactly the atmosphere in which I love to work and collaborate." His contract stipulated a $15,000 salary (about $171,000 today) and the virtually unheard-of proviso that he could later turn his score into a concert suite over which he would exert full control of the rights. Such was Bernstein's star power. *On the Waterfront* dominated Bernstein's schedule from February to May. He wrote, "Day after day, I sat at a Moviola [a foot pedal–controlled device in use since the 1920s that allows a film editor to repeatedly view a movie on a small screen and make cuts], running the print back and forth, measuring in feet the sequences I had chosen for music, converting feet into seconds by mathematical formula, making homemade cue sheets. And every time, I wept at the same speeches, chuckled at the same gestures." Bernstein, who has said that he studied the movie in whole or in part at least 50 times while working on the score, created 48 minutes of music for what would go on to become a 108-minute motion picture.

He devised three major overarching themes. For the movie's opening moments, he laid down a theme presaging Terry Malloy's slow march toward a kind of heroism and redemption. Orchestrated for a noble, mournful solo French horn joined later by a flute and, eventually, a trumpet, to Bernstein it was "a quiet representation of the tragic nobility that underlies the surface of the main character." A second theme—percussive, angry, aggressive—dramatizes the urban jungle–style violence of the New Jersey docks, mostly conveyed by what Bernstein proscribed in his music charts as a jangly saxophone with a "dirty sound." In its power, it anticipates the gang violence themes of *West Side Story* three years later. The third theme (Bernstein titled it "The Glove Theme") gets introduced during Edie and Terry's conversation and tentative flirtation as they walk through the park. To be orchestrated with a flute and strings, it's as lyrical and filled with longing as anything Bernstein would go on to write for Maria and Tony in *West Side Story*. Another romantic moment, when Terry shyly asks Edie out, restates the love (or "Glove") theme, this time with a full and soaring orchestral feel. It feels like the most cinematic of any of the themes.

Much of the score flies in the face of Hollywood's penchant for bombast, but it is an insistent score. And there is lots and lots of it. For instance, for the heart-wrenching scene of Terry's discovering his beloved pigeons slaughtered by his young friend Tommy, Bernstein's music cue runs over five minutes. For the final minutes of the film—when the battered, "crucified" Terry staggers back to work to live another day—Bernstein spotted over four minutes of music. He didn't set out to tell the audience what to feel. He deepened and ennobled what he knew they would already be feeling. Said Karl Malden, who had watched Brando film with the pigeons, the actor's special gifts became impossible to overlook: "There was something Marlon did with those pigeons that I don't think any other actor could do. He loved them. You knew that he loved them. He was just beautiful with that. . . . That was something." Bernstein felt it, and what he did with the underscoring, that, too, was something.

Over three long April daytime sessions on a Columbia Pictures recording soundstage, Morris Stoloff, Columbia Pictures' music director since 1936, recorded the score. A shrewd businessman known for giving composers wide berth, Stoloff worked smoothly with Bernstein, who elected to be present at the recording sessions while letting Stoloff handle the technical aspects of marrying the score with the images. News of the sessions made quite a splash. Among those present was Herschel Burke Gilbert, who composed scores for numerous TV series and films, including *It Came from Beneath the Sea* and *Beyond a Reasonable Doubt*. He said, "Everybody talked about Lenny Bernstein was coming to do a score in Hollywood. What would he do?" The orchestra, at its fullest, featured 47 musicians—a sizable but not overly lavish number of players. The lineup of musicians included French horn player James Decker, the soloist heard on those haunting and searching opening notes of the score. Decker, whose film work spans from *Leave Her to Heaven* in 1945 to *The Star Chamber* in 1983, thought Bernstein's *On the Waterfront* score refreshingly atypical. Said Decker, "The opening, being what it was, allowed me to do a little phrasing, which is nice. I was able to milk it a little bit. You don't get that chance much in the studios." Bernstein stuck around for the entire sessions, even playing a low-down bluesy piano for the bar dance scene between Brando and Saint. For that little bit of business, he received $48.21, union scale.

Easily the biggest bone of contention regarding the finished score centered on the taxicab scene between Terry and his Judas-like brother, Charley. Kazan thought Schulberg's writing and the performances of Marlon Brando and Rod Steiger were so strong that the scene could stand on its own without the underscoring. Bernstein vehemently disagreed and wrote four minutes of music—deeply mournful, elegiac, and aching with loss and with a looming sense of death. When Kazan heard Bernstein's music for the scene, he agreed to leave in some of the taxi music—at least until the film previewed. Meanwhile, Harry Cohn and his other Columbia executives worried far less about the quality of Bernstein's score than whether his political views and affiliations would explode in damaging headlines that could jeopardize the release of their movie. J. Edgar Hoover's FBI had been surveilling and compiling files on Bernstein since 1939. Over the next decade, the bureau's internal memos sounded the alarm about his liberal politics and support of such groups as the Joint Anti-Fascist Refugee Committee, the Southern Negro Youth Congress, the Civil Rights Congress, and the American Committee for Yugoslav Relief, all of which were deemed to be seething with so-called Soviet and Communist influences. Not only politically progressive but also bisexual, Bernstein became one of the obsessions of Joseph McCarthy, the performative, attention-hungry senator from Wisconsin hell-bent on finding a Communist under (or in) every bed. His clownish televised tantrums and lunacies would have been patently ridiculous and pathetic if they hadn't led to the destruction of the careers of so many artists and entertainers. By 1951, Bernstein was labeled a "Communist" in the FBI Security Index, meaning that as an "enemy sympathizer," he could be arrested and held indefinitely in a detention camp in the event of a national emergency. The Department of State denied renewal of his passport in 1953 until Bernstein expressed regret for signing petitions and showing support for "Communist front" organizations. Despite the government's amassing 600 pages of "evidence" of Bernstein's sympathies, the FBI never managed to get their man, nor was he called before the HUAC. But on August 3, 1953, Bernstein hoped to clear his name and regain his passport by submitting a lengthy, self-castigating affidavit. The document, characterized as "a humiliating confession of political sin" by author Barry Seldes, made its impact. Days later, Bernstein's passport got renewed. Still, Cohn wondered if the shoe would drop and cause problems for the movie.

## The First Screening

The first showing for cast members and the filmmakers took place at the venerably utilitarian Magno Screening Room at 729 Seventh Avenue in midtown Manhattan. Among those present were Elia Kazan, Marlon Brando, Leonard Bernstein, and Sam Spiegel. When the lights came back up after the screening, Brando was so disheartened by what he saw as his "huge failure" that he slipped silently out of the theater. Later, he confessed to Karl Malden that his portrayal depressed him because others would see that he was inconsistent and "in and out" of his scenes as Terry. He brooded over why his former mentor and friend Kazan hadn't guided and pushed him more effectively. "Not a word, not even a goodbye," Kazan wrote later about Brando vanishing from the screening so unceremoniously.

Meanwhile, Spiegel failed to accurately read the room's stunned silence at the final fadeout. He interpreted the muted reactions as downbeat responses to the film. "This is a great picture!," he could be heard shouting to no one in particular as the invitees trickled out of the theater and into the lobby. Kazan bristled when he overheard Spiegel trying to assuage Bernstein's anger over how he thought his score was misused. Although Bernstein won the battle over whether the taxi scene played better with music, he would not accept Kazan's attempts to console him. Shortly before the movie was set to open at the Astor Theater at 57 Broadway at West 45th Street in New York City, Bernstein took his grievances public with a *New York Times* essay. He wrote of how "frustrating and maddening" it was to hear his score become barely audible at times or cut off mid-phrase or otherwise mishandled: "I found myself pleading for a beloved G-flat. Sometimes the music, which had been planned . . . with a beginning, middle and end, would be silenced seven bars before the end." The *Times* essay included this final line, which seemed insincere and overly upbeat even for 1954, "It was a glorious experience. I wouldn't have missed it for anything." Interestingly, Bernstein reprinted a much longer version of the essay in his 1959 book *The Joy of Music*. That final line was conspicuously missing.

Despite the critical acclaim Bernstein would receive for *On the Waterfront*, he would spurn decades of offers to score another film.

## Publicity: "*Going My Way . . .* But with Brass Knuckles"

Once again, Sam Spiegel was awash in flop sweat. From his producer's point of view, there wasn't much to exploit the film's still being titled *Waterfront* or *The Waterfront* that seemed . . . well . . . sexy. In the absence of what Spiegel called "exploitable elements," the voluble Budd Schulberg—who resented screenwriters' tending to get short shrift from the press—was only too willing to meet the press. Meanwhile, Spiegel, himself desperate for cash, offered his services to help sell the movie. Even with creditors poised to seize his remaining assets, Spiegel was incredulous when Columbia offered him $500 a week to meet the press. "I tip waiters more than that," he responded. But it was Brando the press was after. But the beleaguered star reluctantly agreed to do very few interviews with entertainment reporters, for whom he often expressed contempt—veiled and otherwise. And not without reason, at times. Consider what was printed of his conversation with *The Daily News* movie critic and columnist Wanda Hale, who reported that the movie "records actual events [but] the boy and girl roles were created for bigger box-office returns. Columbia expects *The Waterfront* to take hold of audiences' emotions in much the same way as the company's 1953 prize winning drama *From Here to Eternity*." Brando described Terry Malloy to Hale as "all mixed up, bewildered, trying to decide between what's right, what's wrong. He is basically a good boy, not conscious that he is on the wrong side until he meets the girl and the priest. Through their influence, he discovers his own decency and courage."

The editors of *Life* magazine featured Eva Marie Saint on their cover for July 19, 1954 ("From TV to Stardom in Movie *Waterfront*"), without offering a single quote from the reticent actress. But Spiegel and the Columbia publicity department took heart from the magazine's observation: "Elia Kazan's brilliant *On the Waterfront* is the most brutal movie of the year, but it also contains the year's tenderest love scenes. Responsible for both violence and romance is Marlon Brando who gives his finest film performance to date. He gets . . . sensitive support in the love department from a new discovery from TV, Eva Marie Saint . . . [as] a convent-reared child of the slums." Six years before, *Life* had featured the then-unknown Saint, its writer predicting, "The name of Eva Marie Saint may someday be a household word like Bankhead, Bergman or [joking for the sake of alliteration] (Milton) Berle." In puff pieces, Kazan built up Saint as "sweet without being coy, nice without being dull and beautiful without being a beauty."

With the decision to release the film under the title *On the Waterfront*, Kazan and Spiegel oversaw the creation of a trailer, using Bernstein's music cues, the copy for which almost read like a review: "The management of this theater believes that *On the Waterfront* is one of the truly great pictures of our time. Superb acting, inspired direction and a story that is as warm and moving as *Going My Way* (but with brass knuckles!) make *On the Waterfront* an achievement that will long be remembered as great motion picture entertainment. We urge you to see it." The trailer hypes Marlon Brando "in a towering performance as Terry Malloy" and "introducing Eva Marie Saint in an unforgettable screen debut."

The trailer promises "tender love . . . terrifying conflict . . . exalted frenzy! Mark down *On the Waterfront* as one motion picture you must see!" The cast and scenes of sex, violence, and action were pushed rather than the past achievements of, say, Kazan or Brando. But Columbia's marketing department created posters and newspaper ads featuring Brando looking warily over his shoulder and his name big, bold, and solo over the title. The ad copy read: "A poignant love story . . . the world's toughest stretch of waterfront . . . and a picture that may well be one of the all-time greats! . . . Tenderness and terrifying conflict in another masterful drama from the star-director of *A Streetcar Named Desire* actually filmed along the world's roughest waterfront!"

Columbia hoped that Schulberg would take up the slack when it came to publicizing the film. But the writer could not be buttoned up. Never having forgiven the way Darryl F. Zanuck treated him and Elia Kazan, on July 11, 1954, roughly two weeks before *On the Waterfront* opened in theaters in the United States, *The New York Times* published the feature article penned by Schulberg. The story was meant to publicize the movie, but Schulberg, being Schulberg, wrote, without once mentioning Zanuck by name: "The head of the studio had changed his mind. *Waterfront* wouldn't fit in with the program of costumed horse operas he was lining up. . . . The picture was still too controversial, we were told. Too grim, too shocking. And would the people care about the struggle on the docks?" Putting the finest possible point on it, Schulberg accused the unmentioned Zanuck of losing "his courage and [running] out on a 'touchy' subject."

Exactly one month before the movie was set to open in New York City on July 28, 1954, Elia Kazan also sent Zanuck a long letter in which he dredged up his residual animosity over the studio boss's rejection of *On the Waterfront*. Hollywood feuds don't die; they fester. Not surprisingly, on July 15, four days after Budd Schulberg got things off his chest in his *New York Times* article, Zanuck replied to Kazan's letter with a missive of his own marked "Personal and Confidential." Zanuck's letter read like one long clapback: "You have a short memory, Gadg. Budd came to see me more than once. I spent many hours on many days working with him and trying to develop and alter the script. He accepted all but one of my major suggestions. You accepted them. Four of them are part of your finished picture, or at least I have been told so by those who have seen the picture and who also had read the original treatment and script and had also read the conference notes."

Warming to his theme, Zanuck continued, "I am really astonished that Budd should write anything such as this. Even more than this, he knows how I sweated and worked with him in a conscientious effort to improve the dramatic construction of the story, and particularly the love story, etc., etc. The last day I saw him he shook my hands and told me that no matter how it turned out he had received valuable assistance and that working with me had been a 'unique and exhilarating experience.'" Zanuck assured Kazan that he was not asking for screen credit but wrote, "I am asking of both Budd and you that you treat me fairly and that you recognize the facts."

In the end, though, Zanuck blamed his decision not to finance the movie on—"more than anything else"—the economic necessity of Cinemascope, which was 20th Century Fox's answer to such other innovations as 3D and three-panel widescreen Cinerama, merely two of Hollywood's frantic attempts to stem the tide of regular moviegoers defecting to television as their primary source of entertainment. Zanuck explained that he felt "that since we had overnight committed ourselves to a program of Cinemascope 'spectacles,' I had no alternative but to back away from intimate stories even though they were good stories. I have since changed my mind as one of our most successful pictures is based on an intimate story." He's referring to the glossy box-office success *Three Coins in the Fountain*, his idea of an "intimate story," in which American women working in Italy find love and heartbreak while meandering through interminable, photogenic travelogue footage of Rome and Venice.

Zanuck goes on to congratulate Kazan on making what he hears is a "wonderful" picture, "every great picture is helpful to the best interests of our industry." He closes by mentioning that he has sent the same letter to Schulberg because "I just cannot accept the idea that I lost my courage or gave you a quick brush-off." He invites Kazan to visit him when the director has finished making *East of Eden* with James Dean at Warner Bros. "You and I are due for a hit next time we get together," he adds in closing, alluding to their most recent collaboration, John Steinbeck's *Viva Zapata!*, which was not a financial success. Kazan would never again make a film for 20th Century Fox or Zanuck.

Now it was time for *Waterfront* to face the public.

SEVEN

# Flop Sweat When Facing the Nation

*O*n *the Waterfront* opened at the Astor Theater on July 28, 1954.
Kazan turned up at the Times Square theater to see if anyone was there for the 11:00 a.m. showing, the day's first. When he
saw roughly 100 ticket buyers in line, he reckoned the movie might
have a shot. No wonder. A stark, brutal, realist drama with a black-
and-white documentary-style aesthetic certainly had to look like a
unicorn among that summer's other big-screen openings, including
biblical epics, sagebrush shoot- 'em-ups, suspense melodramas, and
lush, romantic tearjerkers. From the vantage point of 2024, it may
seem disingenuous to hear that anyone involved with *On the Waterfront* would have doubted the quality of the work, let alone their
work in it. Surely, they *must* have known they had made something
special. "That's a myth," said Rod Steiger. "The actor is so busy just
hoping he can do it. He knows one thing in general. It's a very good
script, a powerful script—good actors, good director. And that's
all. You can't judge yourself in life, whether you're an actor or not.
You just go one moment at a time, one scene at a time. When I saw
[*On the Waterfront*], I thought it was a very good movie. But today,
sometimes I feel that if I see the taxi scene one more time, I'll shoot
myself. This scene has become identified as, supposedly, one of the
great scenes in cinema."

The night of the opening, those involved in the production had at least some cause for optimism. A July 6 sneak preview for the press and the public at the 2,500-seat Loew's Lexington Theater at 571 Lexington Avenue had gone much better than expected. In the audience that night was New Jersey–born 24-year-old songwriter, singer, and record producer Bob Crewe, who would years later create million-selling signature tunes for Frankie Valli and the Four Seasons. Said the die-hard movie fan, who would later become a close friend of the third and last Mrs. Sam Spiegel, Betty, to whom the film mogul was married from 1957 until Spiegel's death in 1985, "The movie stunned the audience, it was such a brutal slice of life. We hadn't seen movies like that outside of the Italian import films of the day. The crowd went crazy when Brando got up on his feet after getting beaten to a pulp. They cheered like they were seeing an old Warner Bros. gangster movie. Brando's performance was electrifying. He had Montgomery Clift's sensitivity but he radiated sex in a way that even Clift and James Dean didn't. I recall people leaving the theater speechless."

Newspaper reviews poured in immediately following the press preview. A surprising and impressive thing about the reviews—especially in our current era of crediting directors with virtually *everything*—is how widespread was the attention paid to journalist Malcom Johnson's Pulitzer-winning investigative reporting and to Budd Schulberg's screenplay. To the latter point, the (unidentified) *Variety* critic led off by saluting Schulberg's "expertly turned, colorful and incisive dialog" long before going on to hail Brando for his "spectacular" and "fascinating, multi-faceted performance." Also on the money is the *Variety* critic's detecting the movie's indebtedness to earlier genre movies, noting its "strong accent on murder and mayhem somewhat reminiscent of the picturized gangsterism of the 1920s (per early James Cagney)" and calling such images as Rod Steiger's corpse pinned to a wall by and hanging from a grappling hook as "particularly suggestive of the stark meller [melodrama] stuff of the past era." *Variety's* critic called out, as others would, the finale's "lacking in conviction" and its being "designed for grandstand cheers" and how Bernstein's musical score "at a couple of points pounds its way to the foreground but mostly complements the screen action well enough." Although A. H. Weiler complained in his *New York Times* review about the movie's "happy ending, its preachments and a somewhat slick approach to some of the facets of dockside strife and tribulations," he praised it as "moviemaking of a rare and high order."

*The Hollywood Reporter* critic Jack Moffitt cited Budd Schulberg's script as a "a masterpiece of screen journalism," helping to create "a patriotic and sometimes poetic picture." And in "one of the year's important films," thanks to Kazan's "superb" direction, Moffitt lauded Brando for a performance that "grabs your heart in a calloused fist and never lets go," backed by Saint, who is "just as good as the girl. Her haggard loveliness . . . makes the prettiness of the average starlet seem trivial." He also predicted that the movie—"so stark and gripping that it can only be compared with *Little Caesar* and *The Public Enemy*"—was sure to create "a new vogue for gangster pictures." He praised, in order, Schulberg, Kazan, Brando, Spiegel, Bernstein, and Boris Kaufman for illustrating "the murder and mayhem of the waterfront's sleazy jungles." He gave Brando high marks for a "shatteringly poignant portrait of an amoral, confused, illiterate citizen of the lower depths" for creating "a beautiful and moving portrayal." He responded to Saint's "tenderness and sensitivity to genuine romance" as well as to Malden's performance, although he thought the priest's "importance in the scheme of things seems overemphasized." And he cited the "excellent" newcomer Steiger's final scene with Brando as "a harsh and touching revelation of their frailties."

Actors of the day responded generously to the film. Humphrey Bogart, who appeared that same year in the high-profile movies *Sabrina, The Barefoot Contessa,* and an Oscar-nominated turn in *The*

*Caine Mutiny*, said, "Wrap up all the Oscars, including mine, and send them over to Brando." Peter Ustinov called it "magnificent" and "a picture with a mind behind it. What a relief to see a movie that aims high and hits the mark." Shelley Winters called it "a great movie and tremendous theater." Kirk Douglas thought it was "powerful" and that Brando did "his best job." Directors rushed to praise the movie too, with George Stevens (*A Place in the Sun*) calling Kazan's direction "masterful" and highlighting Brando at "his very best." Otto Preminger (*Anatomy of a Murder*) opined, "Elia Kazan's direction and Marlon Brando's performance will live in my memory forever as a great emotional experience." Joshua Logan (*Picnic*) thought the movie gave Brando "one of the finest actors of our time . . . a fine opportunity to show his extraordinary ability." Mervyn Leroy (*The Wizard of Oz*) called it "the most dynamic motion picture I've ever seen." Ironically, even producers who rejected Kazan and Schulberg's pleas to finance the movie, such as Samuel Goldwyn (*The Best Years of Our Lives*), chimed in to call it an "important, exciting picture, beautifully written, directed and acted."

Critics lavished considerable praise on Bernstein's score. This from *The Hollywood Reporter*: "Leonard Bernstein's mastery of modern musical technique delivers a truly outstanding score." Kazan somehow couldn't even give Bernstein that. He said, "I try not to bring another personality into the picture through the music but there was no way to avoid that with Lenny. So you're aware of the music. It put the picture on the level of almost operatic melodrama here and there."

When the movie opened throughout Europe from early September through October, the international reviews were also strong, typified by critic Brian McArdle's praise in an article in Melbourne, Australia's *The Age* in which he called the movie "expertly made and directed with a passionate belief in its fierce indictment of rackets and their exponents." Summarizing it as "an epitome of America . . . brash, high-powered and technically flaw-less," he called it marked by "perfect teamwork" between Brando and Kazan. The public, much to the delight and relief of Columbia, Spiegel, Kazan, and Schulberg, apparently agreed. In 1954, when an average movie ticket ran 47 cents, *On the Waterfront* brought in $9.6 million ($239 million, adjusted for 2024) at the box office, 10.5 times its production budget of $910,000.

# EIGHT

# Underdogs at the Oscars

The announcement of the 27th Academy Awards marked another high point for the filmmakers. *On the Waterfront* earned 12 nominations, including Best Picture; Best Director; Best Story and Screenplay; Best Actor; Best Supporting Actress; three Best Supporting Actor nominations; Best Cinematography, Black and White; Best Original Score; Best Film Editing; and Best Art Direction, Interior Decoration, Black and White. That year, the Academy Awards ceremony was held on March 30, 1955, with Bob Hope hosting the transcontinental broadcast from the RKO Pantages Theater in Hollywood while Thelma Ritter did the honors from the NBC Theater in New York City.

Of all the unlucky Best Supporting Actor award winners to be tapped to name the Best Supporting Actress of the succeeding year, the unluckiest would appear to be Frank Sinatra—the Terry Malloy that might have been—to whom it fell to announce the very pregnant Eva Marie Saint as Best Supporting Actress. Recalls Saint:

> We didn't think we had a chance, because it wasn't a typical Hollywood film at the time. But all of a sudden, a few people started winning for *Waterfront*. I started getting edgy because I was very pregnant. My husband said, "If you hear your name called, wait ten seconds before you rush up to accept the Oscar." I told him it wasn't going to happen. Then, all of a sudden, I heard

my name called. I couldn't get up, because my husband had his thumb on my thigh, to prevent me from getting up too quickly. Once I got [onstage], I said, "Thank you, I'm so excited I may have the baby right here. But I would love to thank Elia Kazan, Sam Spiegel, Marlon Brando, Karl Malden, Boris Kaufman, all the longshoremen." The interesting thing to me is that in those days all you were supposed to do was come onstage and accept your award and all you had to do was say, "Thank you." You didn't have to be clever or have dialog with another actor. So that's why I liked my speech.

She gave birth 48 hours later.

An amiable, well-behaved Marlon Brando announced Kazan for "Best Direction." In New York, Thelma Ritter handed the statue to Kazan, who said in his acceptance speech, "A director doesn't make a picture, a whole lot of people do. And I thank each one of them. Thank you. Thank you, Marlon." Bette Davis, who had made her first movie in three years, received prolonged applause as she took the stage to announce Brando as the Best Actor for 1955. Said Brando, hefting the award, "It's much heavier than I imagined. I had something to say but I can't remember what I was going to say for the life of me. I don't think that ever in my life have so many people been so directly responsible for my being so very, very glad. It's a wonderful moment and a rare one and I'm certainly indebted. Thank you." Karl Malden handed Budd Schulberg his Academy Award and the screenwriter said, "Karl, thank you very much, and because my old man B. P. Schulberg was a screenwriter back in 1912 (*sic*; actually 1908) and wrote [*Rescued from an Eagle's Nest*] for D. W. Griffith and because a picture he made called *Wings* I think—I think—won the Academy Award for [Best Picture, Production], this little fellow gives me an added kick tonight." He added, shaking Malden's hand, "And thank you very much." Finally, producer Buddy Adler (*From Here to Eternity*) announced *On the Waterfront* as the best film of the year. Sam Spiegel said, "I'm very grateful to all of you. In this year of great achievements in the motion picture industry, all of us who worked on *Waterfront* are deeply appreciative to all of you for the honor, for the confidence, compliments and for the distinction. Thank you very much."

The real drama behind the Oscars, though, was between Sinatra and Brando. The thin-skinned, vindictive Sinatra may have made his version of peace with Spiegel and Kazan, but he still had it out for Brando. Not only had he lost to Brando the *Waterfront* role he so coveted, but he had also just watched the actor accept the Academy Award that might have gone to him. But Sinatra's animosity toward Brando didn't stop there; in fact, it only began there. By the time of the Oscars, Sinatra and Brando were embroiled in a blood feud of epic proportions exacerbated by the circumstances of the movie they were also currently filming together, *Guys and Dolls*, from composer-lyricist Frank Loesser's long-running, Tony award–winning Broadway smash. For months, Sinatra had lobbied long and hard to get cast as suave, charismatic gambler Sky Masterson, a showcase role also chased by Gene Kelly, Dean Martin, and Bing Crosby. Meanwhile, director Joseph L. Mankiewicz also approached Burt Lancaster, Robert Mitchum, Kirk Douglas, and Cary Grant, the latter of whom recommended the nonsinging Brando. Brando wavered—*come on, tough guy Stanley Kowalski or Terry Malloy singing and dancing in a musical?*—until Grant told him, "I suggested you for the part. Frank Sinatra desperately wants the role. I hear you don't like Sinatra. Take the role to piss him off."

When Brando expressed to Mankiewicz his fears about making a fool of himself by tackling a musical, the director said, "I've never done a musical either. Let's figure it out together." Brando took the role with the understanding that a pro would dub his singing voice. As Cary Grant predicted, Sinatra, the 20th century's definitive pop crooner, raged at being offered the movie's comic supporting role, Nathan Detroit. It didn't matter that Sinatra's role would be expanded and he would get more songs and scenes than Brando because Brando had bested him again. And worse, Sinatra wouldn't even get to sing "Luck Be a Lady," a Loesser showstopper that he would go on to make a staple of his concert repertoire and could never resist telling the audience while introducing the number, "They had chosen that great baritone of the Metropolitan Opera— Marlon Brando. Holy Jesus. He's a hell of an actor, but when it comes to singing, forget it, Charley."

The *Guys and Dolls* set was a minefield. Brando, horrified to learn that his singing would not be dubbed and he would instead be put through intensive vocal lessons, turned for help and advice to Sinatra. The singer's response? "Look, buddy, I don't go for that Method crap." Chronically thin-skinned and aggrieved, Sinatra also accused Mankiewicz of throwing the movie to Brando, whom the director had come to appreciate while they filmed *Julius Caesar* together in 1953. Sinatra made no attempt to disguise his dislike for Brando, whom he addressed as "Mumbles," another shot at the actor's naturalistic Method-acting style. Sinatra was strictly a one-and-done-style actor who ruthlessly mocked Brando on and off the set for his penchant for exploration and multiple takes. Brando, well behaved up to this point, decided he'd had enough. Shooting a restaurant scene where their characters meet, Brando knew that Sinatra loathed cheesecake, which he was obliged to eat during the scene. In rehearsal, Brando was letter perfect. When filming, he deliberately flubbed the very last line eight different times, forcing Sinatra to eat portions of eight slices of cheesecake. When Brando sabotaged the ninth take, the queasy Sinatra hurled his plate to the floor, stabbed a fork into the table, and bellowed at Mankiewicz, "These fucking New York actors! How much cheesecake do you think I can eat?" Filming the scene the next day, Brando nailed it in one take. Sinatra got the message.

The hostilities reached a fever pitch when, on one of Sinatra's days off, his tempestuous estranged wife, Ava Gardner, visited the

*Guys and Dolls* set, reportedly spending the day with Brando in his private dressing room. Several nights later, Brando got abducted at gunpoint by three men. He reportedly told his friend and sometime stand-in Carl Fiore when he materialized hours later, "One of the goons told me he was going to offer me a choice. He could kill me, a quick and easy death with a bullet in my heart. Or else he'd let me live. If he let me live, he'd castrate me and carve up my face so that no plastic surgeon could ever repair it." The men dropped Brando on the side of the road in the Hollywood Hills, leaving him to flag down a passing car to get back home. Brando explained away his bruises and tense emotional state by telling people that he'd been involved in a motorbike accident. "I've never been so frightened in all my life," he told the friend who was staying at his house when he arrived home at 2:00 a.m.

Although he could never prove Sinatra's involvement in the harrowing abduction, Brando stayed clear of him for the rest of the filming, communicating only through intermediaries, and reportedly hired a bodyguard just in case. So that was the backdrop for Sinatra's and Brando's behavior on and off the Oscar stage. For others involved in *On the Waterfront*, Oscar night and its aftermath were much less clouded by drama. Eight major Oscar wins helped the film become one of its year's top-10 box-office successes. For years, Kazan and Schulberg amused each other by reciting Darryl Zanuck's prediction that a film about "a bunch of sweaty longshoremen" was "exactly what the American people don't want to see." Kazan considered the screenplay "perfect." Schulberg wrote years later that he considered the movie not only a personal triumph but also a triumph for all screenwriters because "just for once, getting a script to the screen in the spirit in which it had been conceived—thanks to that rare director who refused to make a distinction between playwright and screenwright [sic] was victory enough. Find me a director who respects the *play*, as Kazan respected not only this but Bill Inge's,

Tennessee Williams's, or Paul Osborn's, and the *auteur* theory will float away from the hollow, gaseous thing it is. What will remain will be solid screenplays and solid directors who will not only embellish but vivify them."

On the heels of *On the Waterfront* becoming a big moneymaker, a *Los Angeles Times* story reported that Sam Spiegel's profits would now permit him to pay off his IRS debt and regain possession of his 6,000-square-foot house at 702 N. Crescent Driver, Beverly Hills. Spiegel remained irrepressibly larger than life, incorrigible, and full of bravado. A Hollywood story goes that a friend dropped by the Crescent Drive house one morning and told Spiegel that he spotted federal agents gathered outside waiting to pounce on him. "Don't bother me, let me finish my breakfast," Spiegel reportedly answered, finished his breakfast, then escaped out the back door to elude the feds. (In 2022, the same house, owned previously by child star and Oscar nominee turned producer Jackie Cooper, sold for $35 million and was listed as "a teardown"; at the time of this book's publication, the rebuilt property was listed at $7.2 million and is a sprawling 25,000-square-foot, eight-bedroom, eight-bathroom, two-story manse with a 12-car garage and a 12-seat movie theater.)

*On the Waterfront* cemented Spiegel's reputation for the rest of his professional and personal life. On the strength of the movie's success and acclaim, Spiegel was able to leverage such enduring prestige projects as *The Bridge on the River Kwai*, *Lawrence of Arabia*, and *Suddenly, Last Summer*, films that kept him in the game through the 1970s highs and lows of *The Swimmer*, *Nicholas and Alexandra*, *The Chase* (again with Brando), and *The Last Tycoon* (reuniting with Kazan).

At the time of his death at 84 in 1986, Spiegel was convalescing on St. Martin after undergoing prostate surgery in London. He owned a residence on Park Avenue, in London, and on the Riviera. He said in one of his last interviews that he had not "made important pictures in 10 years because I've made them all before. I made five or six of the most classical pictures, concentrated in a short time period. . . . I lived for it; I lived in search of putting all of me into these pictures."

Budd Schulberg hoped that *On the Waterfront* would change minds and hearts and incite true reforms. "*On the Waterfront* was like some of Upton Sinclair's novels," Schulberg told movie critic and author Danny Peary in 2020.

> It helped. It didn't clean up the waterfront. Some days I wish Kazan never came to me to write a movie. I got carried away thinking I could do the same thing in movies as in books. I kept trying to do a film of [Robert F. Kennedy's 1960 book] *The Enemy Within* about the Teamsters Union. I worked years and years and years on it. The mob was too strong and kept it from being done. Another screenplay I worked on with Kazan was about young Puerto Ricans. The most incredible people—we spent so much time listening to their incredible stories. We just fell in love with them. That's the kind of person and director Kazan was. He was willing to spend the time developing this project most people wouldn't have financed. After two and a half years, Sam Spiegel pulled the plug.

But something about which Schulberg remained proud was the 1955 publication of his novel *Waterfront*, written, he said, because "there was so much more to say than a 90-minute movie—even one of the best of them—could possibly suggest." Writing in the realist tradition of Stendhal, Emile Zola, and Theodore Dreiser and positioning the characters from the film in a wider social and historical context, Schulberg bestows full martyrdom on Terry Malloy and instead shifts the focus to Father Barry, the two-fisted "church militant" waterfront priest at odds with the Mob and the church who narrates the story to its grim, nihilistic finale. The respectfully received novel, republished in the 1980s, brought renewed interest to the Kazan film and to Schulberg's still potent talents.

## NINE

# Back to Before

In July 1993, a manilla envelope from Schulberg landed on the desk of his agent Mickey Feinberg. Feinberg, the veteran Hollywood agent (widely known around town as "Cowboy"), had a disarming Southern drawl and folksy street personality that belied his reputation as a smart, shrewd maverick. He decorated his office walls with antlers and horseshoes and the studded lapel of his suit jacket with a pin celebrating his clients the Grateful Dead. His waiting room was as likely to be packed with other clients such as Lily Tomlin as it might be with edgy types such as Bill Bonanno, the notorious Italian American mafioso godfather turned author, whom Feinberg took on when others wouldn't. In the envelope sent by Schulberg, Feinberg found a 117-page screenplay titled *Back on the Waterfront* written by Budd Schulberg from a story by Budd Schulberg and his son Peter Schulberg. This was news. A major writer was returning to hallowed ground.

The contemporary crime thriller sequel—filled with flashbacks and callbacks to characters and incidents from *On the Waterfront*—centers on what happens when young lawyer Matthew Larkin "agrees to launch a class action suit on behalf of broken down alcoholic veteran longshoreman 'Dubby O'Shea,' who accidentally calls Matt 'Terry' because he reminds him of an old stevedore pal. It seems the New Jersey Mob is up to new versions of its old tricks—this time swindling dockworkers out of millions of dollars in pension money.

Matt has only begun digging into the case when Dubby turns up dead, murdered for knowing and talking too much. Warns a character, 'Down here, you either go along—or go away.' Matt is haunted by Dubby's passion for justice and his last words, 'Goddamit, I'm so fulla this thing, I'm ready t' boist with what I fuckin' seen.'" Something Dubby saw was his old friend Terry Malloy getting ambushed and abducted by Johnny Friendly's henchmen, who "crucify him before dumping his body in a marsh." From there, Matt investigates what Dubby has seen, and all the corruption appears to revolve around a smooth-talking, expensively dressed Gotti-style gangster called "Candy"—the kind of thug who pays to have hospitals named after him and bribes city officials to look the other way when he buys up the docks for pennies so he can replace them with high-rise apartments, trendy restaurants, and boutique shops. His pockets get lined, and the locals get pushed into homelessness. Matt's obsessive snooping becomes even more dangerous when he falls in love with a hard-luck, ambitious young widow and mother while learning that he himself is the illegitimate son of Terry O'Malley and Edie Doyle. Edie, married to a straight arrow, churchgoing Knights of Columbus type who knows nothing of her past, reveals the agonizing decision that forced her to put up Matt for adoption when her father rejected her after the unsolved, uninvestigated murder of Terry. Terry, she says, was from "another life"; overcome with emotion, she gives Matt his father's old work jacket as a keepsake.

Matt, inspired by what he learns about his father from survivors of the old waterfront days, takes a leave of absence from his practice, rents an apartment in Red Hook, and launches a crusade to expose on live television a powerful mobster for the monster he is. Of course, our hero's efforts result in violent blowback and painful repercussions—the bombing of his girlfriend's aunt's neighborhood bodega; the car bombing that kills his adoptive mother; and the reemergence of Father Barry, now a broken man and alcoholic, in and out of an Oyster Bay facility for "problem priests." Reveals the priest, "What I said and what I did back then won me a lot of friends in the rank-and-file . . . and plenty of enemies in other places. High places. The next thing I knew, the Waterfront Priest didn't have a waterfront anymore. I was up in Schenectady running bingo games for the ladies' auxiliary." Burdened by the weight of guilt he feels for having "killed Terry, not with my bare hands" but killed him, he confesses to Matt, by "pushing and pushing him until he was so far out in front, he was a sitting duck for Johnny's boys. . . . He fought like and died like a champ—crucified for what he believed. God almighty, if Terry hadn't died, they would have been married. And you, Matt, you . . ."

Against all odds, Matt bravely confronts the gangsters in their lair, shouting, "I'm walking in . . . I'm walking in for Terry Malloy." He and Father Barry emerge victorious, with the priest reigniting his old fire and whipping the angry, dispossessed Red Hook locals into a lynch mob frenzy by railing against "these Draculas in their $2000 suits and hundred thousand dollar mansions sucking your blood, selling blood out of the clinic, looting your pensions, ripping off die-hards like Dubby O'Shea and pushing you to sell your old neighborhood out from under you. When they knock off Dubby, when they try to toss a 'shtarker' [Yiddish for a big shot] like [shopkeeper] Aunt Toni into the fire, then you don't have to wait for Sunday mass to feel the nails of the Crucifixion—Candy Candolo is driving them into you right here on River Steet. This is my church right here where too many good men get crucified—not in some faraway land like you read about in the prayer-book but right where we're standing!" It's meant to be a barnburner of a monologue, the sort of thing that might attract Karl Malden to reprise his famous role and who knows, possibly earn another Oscar nomination? Likewise, Schulberg wrote several emotionally charged scenes for Edie that might have tempted Eva Marie Saint back to the world of one of her biggest successes.

"That was the idea but we never got that far," says writer-producer John Watson (*Robin Hood: Prince of Thieves* and *Backdraft*), who was initially contacted about the project by former publicist, super-agent, and Columbia Pictures boss Guy McElwaine, to whom Schulberg's agent had sent the screenplay. Recalls Watson of working with Budd Schulberg on a story outline and two screenplay drafts:

> I'd be lying if I said that I've seen *On the Waterfront* many times and that it had a huge impact on me. I liked it. I admired it. But I jumped at the chance to meet Budd. I thought this one had a shot. It was fresh, had strong characters, had something to say and it was a sequel to a much-beloved film. Budd was still a terrific writer but I thought they might bring in a new writer to give it a fresh-up because the dialogue was slightly on the nose. To be blunt, I don't think Columbia was serious about it. It just seemed to me that they didn't feel they could say no to Budd, made a cheap deal with the thought, "Let's see what we get." I think what they got was and is pretty damn good. I felt so bad when I had to call Budd and tell him that they didn't want to go ahead with it. It was probably shattering to him that his call to glory went unheard and unwanted.

Shattered or not, Schulberg, two years later in 1995, made a headlong rush at a $3 million Broadway version of *On the Water-front*. Acknowledging the high stakes, Schulberg told reporters at the time, "As far as I'm concerned, the main reason for doing the play is to tell that story of what the priest went through as a result of his work on the waterfront—we didn't have time to get into that in the movie. He caught as much hell as the kid did. Now, the roles are virtually equal." Who but Schulberg would think that what *On the Waterfront* needed more of onstage or onscreen was Father Barry? In any event, *New York Times* film critic Vincent Canby described the production as "what happens when a Rolex of a film is taken apart for no special esthetic reason, then put back together with much of its mechanism missing." *Los Angeles Times* theater critic Laurie Winer, calling the show "a depressingly obvious affair," opined, "A new dramatic version of *On the Waterfront* opened at the Brooks Atkinson on Monday night. 'Why?' The story is a moral primer, self-righteous, creaky and loaded with more Christian symbolism than *The Grapes of Wrath* and *The Bad Lieutenant* combined." The play seemed cursed from the outset. During rehearsals and previews, the original director exited, and a new one rushed in at the 11th hour, an actor playing a corrupt union thug who had suffered a heart attack during the final preview. Then, David Morse was brought in to replace Terry Kinney in the role of Father Barry, whom Winer described as "not an interesting character—he's simply a person exhorting everyone to do the right thing all the time and is a mouthpiece for some of Schulberg's most self-conscious writing." David Letterman lampooned the show on his top 10 list, and a cartoon in the *New York Post* depicted the cast and the producers leaping off a pier. The show closed after only eight performances and lost $2.6 million, a record loss for a nonmusical.

Schulberg and Stan Silverman's rewritten version of the play opened to a much better response on February 12, 2009, at London's Haymarket Theatre. Directed by and featuring Steven Berkoff as Johnny Friendly, the production drew nearly unanimously positive reviews. The critic for *The Evening Standard* hailed it as "a thrilling work of art" while *The Guardian* called it "a gripping piece of theater." Schulberg seemed poised to reclaim his ability to stir hearts and minds with *Back on the Waterfront*. But he died on August 2, 2009, and that possibility was denied him.

Eva Marie Saint enjoyed a long, storied career onstage, in films, and on television and never stopped being asked about Brando and

*Waterfront.* She recalled, "I only saw him once after *On the Waterfront.* Years later, Elizabeth Taylor was having a birthday party and he came into the room—I was so excited to see him. He came up, we hugged, and he saw a young brunette over my shoulder. He said good-bye and that was the last time I ever saw him. Somewhere along the way, he lost the love of acting. I mean, look what he did to his instrument. All you have is your instrument, like a musician has his instrument. You take care of it. He moved to a mountaintop. I don't know why. But it was our loss."

# TEN

# Kazan Goes Back to the Oscars

*O*n *the Waterfront* remained the high and low point of Elia Kazan's career. In 1997, when he was 87, the American Film Institute declined for the third time to honor him with a Life Achievement Award. The Los Angeles Film Critics Association did the same. The decision provoked major dissension within the critics' ranks and moved a longtime *Variety* journalist to write about Kazan as "an artist without honor in his own country, a celebrated film maker whose name cannot be mentioned for fear of knee-jerk reactions of scorn and disgust, a two-time Oscar winner not only politically incorrect but politically unacceptable according to fashion and the dominant liberal-left Hollywood establishment." The vice president of the Los Angeles Film Critics Association countered, "When you're honoring someone's entire career you're honoring the totality of what he represents, and Kazan's career, post 1952, was built on the ruins of other people's careers. Ironically, Kazan's films became richer and more morally complex after he informed. But to give our highest award to him would be ignoring a serious moral issue. We would be passively saying, 'We don't care if people inform on their colleagues.'" When Kazan was asked if he were troubled by the degree of controversy and anger his name provoked, he said, "You want to know the truth? Not one bit. I've had so much praise in my

life. Some of it was deserved, some of it not. What does it matter?"
Of his McCarthy-era testimony to the House panel, he remained
as unapologetic as ever: "That whole time wasn't very nice. People
were really hurt by what went on. I was part of it, I suppose. I spoke
my mind and I had a right to do it."

Two years later, Hollywood demonstrated its lingering ambivalence toward Kazan when, at the suggestion of Karl Malden, the
Academy of Motion Picture Arts and Sciences chose to give the
director an Honorary Award. Outside the theater on the day of the
awards ceremony on March 21, 1999, protestors in the hundreds—
some of them blacklisted writers and their family members—hoisted
signs reading "Kazan—Snitch" and "Elia Kazan—Benedict Arnold."
Also in the crowd were counterprotestors, in part organized by the
Ayn Rand Institute, chanting and holding signs reading "Thank you,
Kazan, for not being silent" and "Hollywood communists supported
Stalin." Onstage, co-presenters Martin Scorsese and Robert De Niro
introduced Kazan as a "poetic realist" and "angry romantic" who
"spoke fervently to our most basic conflicts—between races and reli-
gions, classes and generations, men and women." As Kazan slowly
crossed the stage to both applause and catcalls, audience members
Meryl Streep, Warren Beatty, Kurt Russell, Kathy Bates, and others joined in a standing ovation while Nick Nolte sat with his arms
crossed and Ed Harris and Amy Madigan pointedly refrained from
applauding. Kazan simply said, "I thank you very much. I really
like to hear that. And I want to thank the Academy for its courage,
generosity. I thank you all very much. I think I can just slip away."
Actor Charlton Heston said at the time, "To deny a filmmaker of Elia
Kazan's abilities, to deny him the [award] is not only petty but shocking." At a later news conference, Academy president Robert Rheme
was pressed to address the controversy at a news conference and said
that the award was solely an endorsement of Kazan's work.

Old wounds may never heal. In 2023, during a panel for the HBO film *The Plot Against America*, the director's granddaughter Zoe Kazan was asked about her grandfather's McCarthy-era actions. She said, "I will say that I thought a lot about how the history of our country affected my family's history, what it meant for my grandfather as an immigrant to this country to have his Americanness tested and the choice that he made from that." Not long before Budd Schulberg died, he told reporters that it was time to forgive Kazan. His admonition was clear and simple: "Remember the work—and *On the Waterfront* is a great work—but forget the politics." In our day of an attempted coup by an outgoing president and his supporters, foreign countries tampering with national election results, elected politicians praising and openly colluding with and taking marching orders from dictators, and the virulent resurgence of racism, antisemitism, hate speech, and fascism, perhaps our better angels might inspire us to remember the work and forgive. But to forget or excuse the politics that ended careers, drove people to suicide, and besmirched reputations? That may asking far too much.

# On the Waterfront

# The Locations

I n the moviemaking era when even exterior scenes were filmed on soundstages, Elia Kazan knew that power and dynamism of Budd Schulberg's *On the Waterfront* screenplay cried out for filming on authentic locations. Today, Hoboken, New Jersey, where Kazan and company filmed virtually all of the movie, is like another world. But recognizable locations remain and regularly draw film lovers back to the waterfront.

1. The shipping docks
2. Downtown, between Fourth and Fifth Streets, between the American Export and Holland America docks
3. Ship's hold scene
4. Red Hook, Brooklyn
5. Father Barry's church
6. Our Lady of Grace, 400 Willow Avenue (exteriors)
7. Church of St. Peter and Paul, 400 Hudson Street (interiors)
8. Waterfront Commission courtroom scene
9. Hoboken City Hall (interior)
10. Roof and pigeon scenes
11. Hudson Street

12. The area once dubbed the "Barbary Coast" for its raucous dive bars, which is now a stretch of high-rise residences and retail store
13. Park and "Glove" scenes, movie magic combined Elysian Park (Hudson Street between 10th and 11th), Stevens Park (Hudson Street), and Church Square Park (400 Garden Street).
14. Terry and Edie's "first date" steakhouse/bar scene
15. Dino & Harry's Truck "pursuit" scene, Court Street cobbled alleyway, which runs from Newark to Seventh Streets

## APPENDIX B

# *On the Waterfront*
# Selected Credits

### Director

Elia Kazan (1909–2003) *A Tree Grows in Brooklyn* 45, *Gentleman's Agreement* 47, *A Streetcar Named Desire* 51, *Viva Zapata!* 52, *On the Waterfront* 54, *East of Eden* 55, *Baby Doll* 56, *A Face in the Crowd* 57, *Wild River* 60, *Splendor in the Grass* 61, *America, America* 63, *The Last Tycoon* 76

### Producer

Sam Spiegel (aka S. P. Eagle) (1901–1985) *Tales of Manhattan* 42, *The Stranger* 46, *The Prowler* 51, *The African Queen* 51, *On the Waterfront* 54, *The Bridge on the River Kwai* 57, *Suddenly, Last Summer* 57, *Lawrence of Arabia* 62, *The Swimmer* 68, *Nicholas and Alexandra* 71, *The Last Tycoon* 76, *Betrayal* 83

### Writers

Malcolm Johnson (1904–1976) Investigative journalist of the 1940s and 1950s, Pulitzer Prize winner (1949) "Crime on the Waterfront"

Arthur Miller (1915–2005) *All My Sons* 48, *Death of a Salesman* 51, *The Crucible (Les sorcières de Salem)*, *The Misfits* 61, *A View from*

176 A City Full of Hawks

*the Bridge* 62, *Playing for Time* 80, *Everybody Wins* 90, *The Crucible* (1996), *National Theater Live: The Crucible* 23

Budd Schulberg (1914–2009) *A Star Is Born* 37, *Nothing Sacred* 37, *On the Waterfront* 54, *The Harder They Fall* 56, *A Fae in the Crowd* 57, *Back on the Waterfront* (unproduced) 93

Robert Siodmak (1900–1973) *People on Sunday* 30, *The Tempest* 32, *Son of Dracula* 43, *Phantom Lady* 44, *Cobra Woman* 44, *The Suspect* 44, *The Strange Affair of Uncle Harry* 45, *The Spiral Staircase* 46, *The Killers* 46, *The Dark Mirror* 46, *Cry of the City* 48, *Criss Cross* 49, *The File on Thelma Jordan* 49, *The Whistle at Eaton Falls* 51, *The Crimson Pirate* 52, *Junie Moon* 70

## Actors

Marlon Brando (1924–2004) *The Men* 50, *A Streetcar Named Desire* 51, *Viva Zapata!* 52, *Julius Caesar* 53, *On the Waterfront* 54 (Terry Malloy), *The Fugitive Kind* 60, *Reflections in a Golden Eye* 67, *The Godfather* 72, *Last Tango in Paris* 72, *Apocalypse Now* 79, *The Score* 2001

Karl Malden (1912–2009) *Charlie Chan at the Opera* 36, *They Knew What They Wanted* 40, *Boomerang* 47, *Kiss of Death* 47, *I Confess* 53, *On the Waterfront* 54 (Father Barry), *Baby Doll* 56, *Fear Strikes Out* 57, *One-Eyed Jacks* 61, *Birdman of Alcatraz* 62, *The Cincinnati Kid* 65, *Billion Dollar Brain* 67, *Patton* 70, *The Streets of San Francisco* (TV) 1972–1977, *Nuts* 87

Eva Marie Saint (1924–) *On the Waterfront* 54 (Edie Doyle), *A Hatful of Rain* 57, *Raintree County* 57, *North by Northwest* 59, *Exodus* 60, *The Russians Are Coming, The Russians Are Coming* 66, *Grand Prix* 67, *Loving* 70, *Nothing in Common* 86, *Mariette in Ecstasy*, 2019

Lee J. Cobb (1911–1976) *The Song of Bernadette* 43, *Golden Boy* 37, *Boomerang!* 47, *On the Waterfront* 54 (Johnny Friendly), *The Man in the Gray Flannel Suit* 56, *The Three Faces of Eve* 57, *12 Angry Men* 57, *Exodus* 60, *How the West Was Won* 62, *Coogan's Bluff* 68, *The Exorcist* 76

Rod Steiger (1925–2002) *Teresa* 51, *On the Waterfront* 54 (Charlie Malloy), *The Big Knife* 55, *Oklahoma!* 55, *The Harder They Fall* 56, *The Longest Day* 62, *Hands Over the City* 63, *The Loved One* 65, *Doctor Zhivago* 65, *In the Heat of the Night* 67, *Mars Attacks!* 96, *Poolhall Junkies* 2002

Leif Erikson (1911–1986) *Show Boat* 51, *Invaders from Mars* 53, *On the Waterfront* 54 (Glover), *Tea and Sympathy* 56, *The Carpetbaggers* 64, *Strait-Jacket* 64, *Mirage* 54, *Twilight's Last Gleaming* 77

Martin Balsam (1919–1996) *Winged Victory* 44, *On the Waterfront* 54 (Gillette), *12 Angry Men* 57, *Middle of the Night* 59, *Psycho* 60, *Breakfast at Tiffany's* 61, *Cape Fear* 62, *Seven Days in May* 64, *A Thousand Clowns* 64, *Hombre* 67, *Catch-22* 67, *The Taking of Pelham One Two Three* 74, *Murder on the Orient Express* 74, *All the President's Men* 76, *Cape Fear* 91, *Legend of the Spirit Dog* 97

Don Blackman (1912–1977) *Two Tickets to Broadway* 51, *Affair in Trinidad* 52, *Champ for a Day* 53, *On the Waterfront* 54 (Luke), *The Egyptian* 54, *The Old Man and the Sea* 58, *Scream Blacula Scream* 73

Rudy Bond (1912–1982) *A Streetcar Named Desire* 51, *On the Waterfront* 54 (Moose), *12 Angry Men* 57, *Butterfield 8* 60, *The Godfather* 72, *The Taking of Pelham One Two Three* 74, *The Rose* 79

Fred Gwynne (1926–1993) *On the Waterfront* 54 (Slim), *Car 54, Where Are You?* (TV) 61–63, *The Munsters* (TV) 64–66, *Simon* 80, *The Cotton Club* 84, *Fatal Attraction* 87, *Ironweed* 87, *Shadows and Fog* 91, *My Cousin Vinny* 92, *Lincoln* 92

James Westerfield (1913–1971) *The Magnificent Ambersons* 42, *The Pride of the Yankees* 42, *Since You Went Away* 44, *On the Waterfront* 54 (Big Mac), *The Shaggy Dog* 59, *Wild River* 60, *The Absent-Minded Professor* 61, *Birdman of Alcatraz* 62, *Man's Favorite Sport?* 64, *Hang 'Em High* 68, *Set This Town on Fire* 73

Tony Galento (aka Tony "Two Ton" Galento) (1910–1979) *On the Waterfront* 56 (Truck), *The Best Things in Life Are Free* 56, *Wind Across the Everglades* 58

Michael V. Gazzo (1923–1995) *On the Waterfront* 54 (Bit), *The Godfather Part II* 74, *Black Sunday* 77, *Fingers* 78, *King of the Gypsies* 78, *Sudden Impact* 83

John F. Hamilton (1893–1967) *The Saint's Double Trouble* 40, *Boomerang!* 47, *On the Waterfront* 54 ("Pop" Doyle)

John Heldabrand (1920–2007) *On the Waterfront* 54 (Mott), *The Wrong Man*, 56

Pat Hingle (1924–2009) *On the Waterfront* 54 (Jocko), *Wild River* 60, *Splendor in the Grass* 61, *The Ugly American* 63, *All the Way* 63, *The Gauntlet* 77, *Norma Rae* 79, *Sudden Impact* 83, *The Falcon and the Snowman* 85, *Batman* 89, *The Grifters* 90, *Batman Returns* 92, *Batman Forever* 95, *Batman and Robin* 97, *Talladega Nights: The Ballad of Ricky Bobby* 2006

Nehemiah Persoff (1919–2022) *On the Waterfront* 54 (Cab Driver), *The Harder They Fall* 56, *The Wrong Man* 56, *Some Like It Hot* 59, *The Greatest Story Ever Told* 65, *Red Sky at Morning* 71, *Voyage of the Damned* 76, *Yentl* 83, *Twins* 88, *Angels in America* 2003

## Crew

### *Art Director*

Richard Day (1896–1972) *Greed* 24, *The Wedding March* 28, *These Three* 36, *Dodsworth* 36, *Stella Dallas* 37, *Dead End* 37, *The Hurricane* 37, *The Hound of the Baskervilles* 39, *The Story of Alexander Graham Bell* 39, *Rose of Washington Square* 39, *Young Mr. Lincoln* 39, *Drums Along the Mohawk* 39, *The Grapes of Wrath* 40, *Lillian Russell* 40, *The Mark of Zorro* 40, *How Green Was My Valley* 41, *Roxie Hart* 42, *The Razor's Edge* 46, *The Ghost and Mrs. Muir* 47, *Miracle on 34th Street* 47, *A Streetcar Named Desire* 51, *On the Waterfront* 54, *Exodus* 60, *The Greatest Story Ever Told* 65, *Valley of the Dolls* 67, *Tora! Tora! Tora!* 70

## Camera Department

Howard Block (1925–2005) *The Naked City* 48, *On the Waterfront* 54, *Bananas* 71, *Godspell* 73, *Melvin and Howard* 80, *Rocky III* 82

Gayne Rescher (1924–2008) *A Face in the Crowd* 57, *Windjammer* 58, *Rachel, Rachel* 68, *A New Leaf* 71, *Claudine* 74, *Melanie Darrow* 97

## Cinematographer

Boris Kaufman (1906–1980) *Zero for Conduct* 33, *Atalante* 34, *Zouzou* 34, *On the Waterfront* 54, *Baby Doll* 56, *12 Angry Men* 57, *The Fugitive Kind* 60, *Splendor in the Grass* 61, *The World of Henry Orient* 64, *The Pawnbroker* 64, *The Group* 66, *Tell Me That You Love Me, Junie Moon* 70

## Makeup

Mary Roche (dates unknown) (hair stylist) *The Heat's On* 43, *On the Waterfront* 54, *Happy Anniversary* 59, *The Fugitive Kind* 60, *Something Wild* 61, *Long Day's Journey into Night* 62

Fred Carlton Ryle (1899–1960) *Jigsaw* 49, *Lost Boundaries* 49, *The Whistle at Eaton Falls* 51, *On the Waterfront* 54, *Singing in the Dark* 56, *Jamboree* 57

Bill Herman (dates unknown) *On the Waterfront* 54, *Murder Inc.* 60, *Fail Safe* 64, *The Pawnbroker* 64, *Lilith* 64

## Production Manager

George Justin (1916–2008) *On the Waterfront* 54, *A Face in the Crowd* 57, *The Goddess* 58, *Inside Daisy Clover* 65, *Up the Down Staircase* 67, *The Graduate* 67, *The Owl and the Pussycat* 70, *Murphy's Romance* 85

# Selected Bibliography

## Books

Alpi, Deborah Lazaroff. 1998. *Robert Siodmak*. Jefferson, NC: McFarland Publishing.

Baer, William, ed. 2000. *Elia Kazan: Interviews (Conversations with Film-makers)*. Minneapolis, MN: University of Minnesota Press.

Bigsby, Christopher. 2009. *Arthur Miller*. Cambridge, MA: Harvard University Press.

Briley, Ron. 2016. *The Ambivalent Legacy of Elia Kazan: The Politics of the Post-HUAC Films*. Lanham, MD: Rowman & Littlefield Publishers.

Burton, Humphrey. 1994. *Leonard Bernstein*. London: Faber and Faber.

Dewey, Donald. 2014. *Lee J. Cobb: Characters of an Actor*. Lanham, MD: Rowman & Littlefield Publishers.

Fisher, James T. 2009. *On the Irish Waterfront: The Crusader, the Movie, and the Soul of the Port of New York*. Ithaca, NY: Cornell University Press.

Fraser-Cavassoni, Natasha. 2003. *Sam Spiegel*. New York, NY: Simon & Schuster.

Gottfried, Martin. 2003. *Arthur Miller: His Life and Work*. Boston, MA: Da Capo Press.

Greco, J. 1999. *The File on Robert Siodmak in Hollywood, 1941–1951*. Dissertation.com.

Grissom, James. 2016. *Follies of God: Tennessee Williams and the Women of the Fog*. New York, NY: Vintage Books.

Huston, John. 1994. *An Open Book*. Boston, MA: Da Capo Press.

Kazan, Elia. 1997. *A Life*. Boston, MA: Da Capo Press.

Kazan, Elia, and Albert J. Devlin. 2014. *The Selected Letters of Elia Kazan*. New York, NY: Alfred A. Knopf.

Malden, Karl. 2004. *When Do I Start?* Honolulu, HI: Limelight Publishing.

Mann, William J. 2020. *The Contender: The Story of Marlon Brando.* New York, NY: Harper Paperbacks.

Mizruchi, Susan L. 2015. *Brando's Smile.* New York, NY: W.W. Norton & Company.

Newman, Paul. 2022. *The Extraordinary Life of an Ordinary Man.* New York, NY: Alfred A. Knopf.

Rapf, Joanna E., ed. 2023. *On the Waterfront.* Cambridge, England: University of Cambridge Books.

Schickel, Richard. 1991. *Brando: A Life in Our Times.* New York, NY: Atheneum.

Schickel, Richard. 1999. *Marlon Brando.* London: Pavilion Books Ltd.

Schickel, Richard. 2005. *Elia Kazan.* New York, NY: HarperCollins.

Schulberg, Budd. 1955. *Waterfront.* New York, NY: Random House.

Schulberg, Budd. 1980. *On the Waterfront: The Final Shooting Script.* Hollywood, CA: Samuel French.

Schulberg, Budd, Haynes Johnson, and Malcolm Johnson. 2005. *On the Waterfront: The Pulitzer Prize–Winning Articles That Inspired the Film and Transformed the New York Harbor.* New York, NY: Chamberlain Brothers.

Seldes, Barry. 2009. *Leonard Bernstein: The Political Life of an American Musician.* Berkeley, CA: University of California.

Simeone, Nigel, ed. 2013. *The Leonard Bernstein Letters.* New Haven, CT: Yale University Press.

Thomson, David. 2023. *Acting Naturally: The Magic of Great Performances.* New York, NY: Alfred A. Knopf.

## Magazines and Blogs

Peary, Gerald. "Film Interview: Budd Schulberg on Being a Screenwriter in Hollywood." The Arts Fuse. August 15, 2020. https://artsfuse.org/209469/film-interview-budd-schulberg-on-being-a-screenwriter-in-hollywood/.

Vonnegut, Kurt. 2001. "Budd Schulberg, The Art of Fiction." *The Paris Review*, 160. https://www.theparisreview.org/interviews/450/the-art-of-fiction-no-169-budd-schulberg.

# Index